Federal Programs and City Politics

This volume is sponsored by the

OAKLAND PROJECT
University of California, Berkeley

Publications in the OAKLAND PROJECT *series include:*

The Politics of City Revenue, by Arnold J. Meltsner, 1971

Implementaton, by Jeffrey L. Pressman and Aaron Wildavsky, 1973

Urban Outcomes, by Frank S. Levy, Arnold J. Meltsner, and Aaron Wildavsky, 1974

Federal Programs and City Politics, by Jeffrey L. Pressman, 1975

Personnel Policy in the City, by Frank J. Thompson, 1975

Federal Programs and City Politics

The Dynamics of the Aid Process

in Oakland

JEFFREY L. PRESSMAN

University of California Press

Berkeley   Los Angeles   London

University of California Press
Berkeley and Los Angeles, California

University of California Press, Ltd.
London, England

Copyright © 1975, by
The Regents of the University of California

ISBN 0-520-02749-3
Library of Congress Catalog Card Number: 74-77733
Printed in the United States of America

To Robert A. Dahl and Aaron Wildavsky,
teachers who made a difference

The Oakland Project

At a time when much is said but little is done about the university's relationship to urban problems, it is useful for those who are looking for ways of relating the university to the city to take a brief look at the Oakland Project of the University of California, which combined policy analysis, service to city officials and community groups, action in implementing proposals, training of graduate students, teaching new undergraduate courses, and scholarly studies of urban politics. The "university" is an abstraction, and as such it exists only for direct educational functions, not for the purpose of doing work within cities. Yet there are faculty members and students who are willing to devote large portions of their time and energy to investigating urban problems and to making small contributions toward resolving them. Our cities, however, do not need an invasion of unskilled students and professors. There is no point in hurtling into the urban crisis unless one has some special talent to contribute. After all, there are many people in city government—and even more on street corners—who are less inept than untrained academics. University people must offer the cities the talent and resources which they need and which they could not get otherwise.

In 1965 a group of graduate students and faculty members

at the University of California at Berkeley became involved
in a program of policy research and action in the neighboring
city of Oakland. As members of the Oakland Project, they tried
to meet some of the city's most pressing analytical needs and
also to make suggestions that could be implemented.

Members of the project made substantial time commitments
(usually about two years) to working in a particular Oakland
city agency. Normal working time was two days a week,
although special crisis situations in the city sometimes necessi-
tated much larger blocks of time. Since project members worked
with city officials and remained in the city to help implement
the suggestions they made, they avoided the "hit-and-run"
stigma that members of city agencies often attach to outsiders.
By attempting first to deal with problems as city officials
understand them, project members developed the necessary
confidence to be asked to undertake studies with broader
implications.

The Oakland Project became a point of communication for
individuals and groups in the city of Oakland and throughout
the University of California. Its focus expanded from a concen-
tration on city budgeting to a wide range of substantive policies
and questions of political process; for example, revenue, police,
personnel, federal aid, education, libraries, and the institutionalization of policy analysis. The Project provided assistance
to governmental (mayor, city manager, chief of police, head
of civil service, superintendent of schools) and nongovernmental (community group) actors. In order to transmit the knowledge gained, Oakland Project members taught courses—open
to both undergraduate and graduate students—dealing with
urban problems and policies. The Project's scholarly objective
is to improve policy analysis by providing new ways of understanding decisions and outcomes that affect cities. Its members
have based numerous research essays on their experience in
the city. It is hoped that the books in this series will be another
means of transmitting what they have learned to a wider
audience.

Contents

ix

Tables

xi

Acknowledgments

I am indebted to many people for stimulation and support during the writing of this book. The initial research was carried out as part of a collaborative action-research effort (the Oakland Project) at the University of California, and I am grateful for the assistance of my colleagues on that project: Frank Levy, William Lunch, Judith May, Arnold Meltsner, Jay Starling, Frank Thompson, and David Wentworth.

On the receiving end of our action-research project was the city of Oakland, where we worked and studied. I would like to thank Mayor Reading and James H. Price (formerly the mayor's administrative assistant and now the area director of the U.S. Department of Housing and Urban Development) for their generosity during all phases of my research.

Special thanks are due to the Berkeley faculty members who supervised my doctoral dissertation, from which much of this book was developed. Aaron Wildavsky, who served as chairman of my dissertation committee, was of invaluable help as a stimulating teacher, as director of the Oakland Project, and as a research colleague. Robert Biller offered many analytical insights that were both original and compelling. And William K. Muir, Jr., often playing the role of a devil's advocate, forced me to sharpen my thinking at a number of points; a complete version of this study would have to include his many intriguing interlinear comments.

After the completion of my dissertation, I carried out additional field research and analysis for the preparation of this book. Particularly helpful in this stage were Bill Cavala, Robert Jervis, Robert Nakamura and, once again, Aaron Wildavsky.

In providing financial support for my research efforts, the Oakland Project was always generous. The project itself was supported by funds first from the National Aeronautics and Space Administration and then from the Urban Institute, under a prime contract from the Department of Housing and Urban Development. For typing various stages of the manuscript, I would like to thank Mary Ellen Anderson, Lucille Flanders, Marcia Raine, and Karen Gourdin (who also contributed editorial suggestions). William J. McClung of the University of California Press has been helpful throughout the writing of this book.

My wife, Kate, has been both a rigorous critic and a builder of my confidence. She has probably engaged in enough conversations about Oakland to last her for many years.

1
Introduction

Federal urban programs—their goals, their structure, and their impact—have constituted a central subject of recent political debate in this country. The future shape of these programs has been an issue in conflicts between the executive branch and Congress, and the signals from Washington have been closely watched by officials at the local level who are the recipients of federal aid. Regardless of the eventual outcome of the struggles over general revenue sharing, special revenue sharing, and categorical programs, it seems clear that the federal government will continue to spend substantial sums of money on urban programs and that both federal and local officials will continue to have an interest in how that money is spent.

Like its foreign aid programs, the United States government's domestic urban aid efforts constitute an attempt to provide financial resources to areas with an acute need for them. But while foreign aid has suffered a decline in appropriations during recent years, urban aid has been increasing. Table 1 shows the sharp rise in federal programs of aid to cities in the years 1961-1972, from approximately $3.9 billion to over $26 billion.

Table 1: Federal Aid Payments in Urban Areas Have
Increased Substantially, 1961–1972

Function and Program	(millions of dollars)			
	1961 Actual	1964 Actual	1969 Actual	1972 Estimate
National Defense	10	28	30	31
Agriculture and Rural Development:				
Donation of Surplus Commodities.	128	231	313	294
Other	27	40	104	81
Natural Resources:				
Environmental Protection........	24	8	79	773
Other	30	10	101	170
Commerce and Transportation:				
Economic Development	0	158	104	147
Highways	1,398	1,948	2,225	2,646
Airports	36	36	83	117
Urban Mass Transportation	0	0	122	289
Other	1	5	5	6
Community Development and Housing:				
Community Action Program	0	0	432	549
Urban Renewal	106	159	786	975
Public Housing	105	136	257	570
Water and Sewer Facilities.......	0	36	52	110
Model Cities	0	0	8	420
Other	3	7	77	704
Education and Manpower:				
Head Start and Follow Through...	0	0	256	97
Elementary and Secondary.......	222	264	1,262	1,457
Higher Education	5	14	210	113
Vocational Education	28	29	179	393
Employment Security Administration	303	344	449	327
Manpower Activities	0	64	530	1,271
Other	3	7	77	704
Health:				
Hospital Construction	48	66	89	113
Regional Medical Program.......	0	0	19	63
Mental Health	4	8	50	66
Maternal and Child Health	18	34	139	203
Comprehensive Health Planning and Services.........	29	48	80	150
Health Educational Facilities	0	0	106	117
Medical Assistance	0	140	1,731	2,074

Function and Program	(millions of dollars)			
	1961 Actual	1964 Actual	1969 Actual	1972 Estimate
Health Manpower	0	0	28	193
Other	0	4	54	283
Income Security:				
Vocational Rehabilitation	37	61	247	400
Public Assistance	1,170	1,450	3,022	5,581
Child Nutrition, Special Milk, and Food Stamps........	131	168	482	1,690
Other	3	16	148	510
General Government:				
Law Enforcement	0	0	17	464
National Capital Region	25	38	85	158
Other	0	9	27	145
Other Functions	0	2	0	5
General Revenue Sharing	0	0	0	2,813*
Total Aids to Urban Areas........	3,893	5,588	14,045	26,848

Source: *Special Analyses, Budget of the United States Government, Fiscal Year 1972*, p. 241.

* Tentative estimated impact calculated on the basis of population includes both direct pass-through and discretionary state allocations.

Through new legislation in the 1960s, Congress extended both the range and level of federal involvement in cities. Major national programs were developed in new fields of activity such as manpower training, and new aid was provided for established local government functions such as mass transportation and sewer and water systems. In both the Economic Opportunity Act of 1964 and the model cities program of 1966, Congress broke with precedent by authorizing aid to local communities for a relatively unrestricted range of functions. And in 1968, the national government initiated a program of aid to local law enforcement—a traditional preserve of local government.[1]

To a large extent, the federal government has tended to bypass the states in establishing and carrying out urban programs. Beginning with education and internal improvement programs in the early nineteenth century, through the emergency public works projects of the 1930s to the community action and model cities programs of the contemporary period,

[1] See James L. Sundquist, with the collaboration of David W. Davis, *Making Federalism Work* (Washington, D. C.: The Brookings Institution, 1969), pp. 1-13, for an introduction to the changing character of federalism.

Washington has created channels of funding that go directly from the national government to the localities.[2] As a rule, states have been slow to develop programs of their own to deal with urban problems, and mayors have generally opposed state interference in federal-local program channels.[3] Because of the growth of direct federal-city programs and the lack of interest shown by most states in these programs, this study will focus on relationships between the federal government and cities.

Stress and Response

As the experience of foreign aid has amply demonstrated, the receipt of outside aid can bring considerable problems, as well as additional financial resources, to the recipient.[4] Like foreign aid, urban aid programs have generated friction between donor and recipient organizations. Federal policy makers have usually diagnosed this friction as stemming from confusion and frustration caused by the fragmentation of federal programs and the lack of communication between federal and city actors. Proceeding from this diagnosis, federal efforts to reduce tensions in the federal system have taken the following forms:

1. *Communication.*—To overcome confusion and lack of information on the part of intergovernmental actors, the federal government has initiated a number of policies designed to increase the information available to these actors and to facilitate communication among them.

In 1959 Congress established a continuing agency for study, information, and guidance in the field of intergovernmental

[2] For historical treatments of the growth of direct federal-city relationships, see W. Brook Graves, *American Intergovernmental Relations* (New York: Charles Scribner's Sons, 1964), pp. 856-883; and Daniel J. Elazar, *American Federalism: A View from the States* (New York: Thomas J. Crowell Company, 1966). The creation of such direct relationships is strongly endorsed by Roscoe C. Martin in *The Cities and the Federal System* (New York: Atherton Press, 1965), p. 82.

[3] Sundquist, *Making Federalism Work*, pp. 261-267.

[4] Some helpful sources on the political impact of foreign aid are John D. Montgomery, *Foreign Aid in International Politics* (Englewood Cliffs, N. J.: Prentice-Hall, 1967); Montgomery, *The Politics of Foreign Aid: American Experience in Southeast Asia* (New York: Praeger Paperbacks, 1962); Eugene B. Mihaly and Joan M. Nelson, "Political Development and U.S. Economic Assistance" (Paper delivered at American Political Science Association Annual Meeting, 1966); Judith Tendler, "Foreign Aid: A Study in Atypical Bureaucracy" and "The Abundance of Foreign Assistance" (Unpublished manuscripts, Department of Economics, University of California at Irvine, 1970).

relations. The permanent Advisory Commission on Intergovernmental Relations, as it is called, is a bipartisan body of twenty-six members who are supposed to represent "governors, mayors, county officials, state legislatures, Congress, the executive branch of the government, and the public at large."[5] The commission derives practically all its financial support from the national government, but it responds "to the needs of all three major levels of government." It does this by encouraging "discussion and study at an early date of emerging public problems that are likely to require intergovernmental cooperation" for their solution.[6]

Presidents have been particularly active in creating institutions for the improvement of federal-local communication. In 1961 President Kennedy established Federal Executive Boards in 10 of the largest cities; by 1969 the number had increased to 25. Board membership was composed of the principal federal civilian and military officials who were located within the designated geographic area. The objectives in creating the boards were to improve communications between Washington and federal field officials and to encourage cooperation among federal agencies. Later, in 1965, the boards were directed to identify unmet urban needs and to devise and carry out intergovernmental efforts to help solve critical urban problems. This task proved impossible; cooperation and communication were no match for the realities of interagency and intergovernmental power. The boards lacked the authority to impose their will on conflicting local and federal organizations.[7]

During the Johnson administration, there was a flurry of activity directed toward the fostering of communication. President Johnson designated Vice President Humphrey to act as his liaison with mayors; the director of the Office of Emergency Planning was to perform the same function with regard to governors. In addition, the Department of Health, Education, and Welfare established an intergovernmental relations staff to maintain direct and continuing contact with local executives.

[5] Richard H. Leach, *American Federalism* (New York: W. W. Norton, 1970).
[6] Advisory Commision on Intergovernmental Relations, *Third Annual Report* (Washington, D. C., 1962), p. 2. Quoted in Leach, p. 50.
[7] Harold Seidman, *Politics, Position, and Power: The Dynamics of Federal Organization* (New York: Oxford University Press, 1970), pp. 179-180.

Finally, in November of 1966, the president issued a memorandum calling on all federal officials to take steps to insure closer
cooperation among federal and local officials. "To the fullest
practical extent," the memorandum read, "I want you to take
steps to afford representatives of the chief executives of state
and local government the opportunity to advise and consult
in the development and execution of programs which directly
affect the conduct of state and local affairs."[8] A Bureau of
the Budget circular subsequently established procedures for
direct consultation between federal agencies and local leaders.

Soon after this communication system was put into effect,
a change in administration resulted in the establishment of
still another framework for cooperation. In 1969, during his
first month in office, President Nixon combined the functions
previously exercised by the Office of Emergency Planning and
the vice president's office by creating an Office of Intergovernmental Relations under the direct supervision of the vice
president. The new office, the president declared, would "seek
to strengthen existing channels of communication and to create
new channels among all levels of government." Furthermore,
the vice president was personally charged with making the
executive branch of the national government "more sensitive,
receptive and responsive" to the views and wishes of local
officials.[9] There appeared to be pervasive support for communication.

2. *Comprehensive Planning*—Once federal and local officials
start communicating with each other, what form—according
to federal pronouncements—should that communication take?
A prime vehicle of intergovernmental conversation is the writing (on the part of the local recipient) and evaluation (on the
part of the federal agency) of a comprehensive plan, which
has become a standard part of the application for urban
funding. Speaking of the poverty program, President Johnson
outlined an ambitious role for planning:

This program asks men and women throughout the country to prepare
long-range plans for the attack on poverty in their own local communi-

---

[8] Leach, *American Federalism*, pp. 178-179.
[9] *Ibid.*, p. 179.

ties. These plans will be local plans calling upon all the resources available to the community—federal and state, local and private, human and material.[10]

Although comprehensive planning requirements were subsequently set aside in the rush to get the poverty program underway,[11] they surfaced gain in the model cities program of 1966. Applicant cities were required to enter into a process of competitive planning. First, they were to submit applications for planning grants that would be evaluated according to fourteen guidelines stated in the president's message on the program. The Department of Housing and Urban Development would judge the potential of each application for changing "the total environment" of the demonstration area and its comprehensiveness in making use of "every available social program."[12] After the proposals were judged, the winning cities would be given another year, and federal funding, to perfect five-year action plans.

Comprehensive planning is designed to encourage local communities to inform themselves about various funding sources and to match those potential resources with the problems they might help solve. In this way, it is hoped that ignorance and confusion about programs can be diminished. But even if local leaders were able to inform themselves completely about available programs and the uses to which they might be put, the leaders would still find that those programs are generated by numerous, fragmented agencies which often work at cross purposes to each other. It is difficult to see how comprehensive planning can make this fragmentation disappear. Something more is needed.

3. *Coordination*—The antidote to fragmentation, expressed in numerous congressional and presidential policy directives, is coordination. For example, in the statute which gave life to the poverty program, Congress authorized the director of that program to "assist the President in coordinating the antipoverty efforts of all federal agencies."[13] In the legislation

[10] Special Message to the Congress on War on Sources of Poverty.
[11] Sundquist, *Making Federalism Work*, p. 81.
[12] Presidential message quoted in *ibid.*, p. 81.
[13] Economic Opportunity Act of 1964, Section 611.

creating HUD, Congress provided that "The Secretary shall ... exercise leadership at the direction of the President in coordinating federal activities affecting housing and urban development."[14] A subsequent executive order directed the secretary of HUD to convene meetings of representatives of all federal agencies whose programs affected cities. Those meetings would "identify urban development problems of particular states, metropolitan areas, or communities which require interagency or intergovernmental coordination."[15]

Other department heads have also been assigned responsibility for coordinating urban programs. An amendment to the Economic Opportunity Act charged the secretaries of Labor and HEW (along with the director of the Office of Economic Opportunity) with "the effective coordination of all programs and activities within the executive branch of the government relating to the training of individuals for the purpose of improving or restoring employability."[16] To supplement this coordination of manpower training programs, an executive order in 1968 boldly announced:

> Cooperative planning and execution of manpower training and supporting service programs is hereby established as the policy of the Federal Government. ... Each department and agency included in CAMPS (Cooperative Area Manpower Planning System) shall participate in manpower coordinating committees at the national and regional levels. The Secretary of Labor shall designate the chairmen of such committees.[17]

President Nixon showed his concern for coordination in the urban field by creating an Urban Affairs Council to "coordinate programs and provide a forum for the discussion of interdepartmental problems that cut across jurisdictions."[18]

Although these attempts at "coordination" are designed to cure the fragmentation of the federal organizational effort in cities, it is obvious that a new phenomenon has been created—

[14] Department of Housing and Urban Development Act (1965), Section 3(b).
[15] "Coordination of Federal Urban Programs," Executive Order 11297, August 11, 1966, Section 1.
[16] Economic Opportunity Act of 1964 (as amended in 1967), Section 637(a).
[17] "Cooperative Area Manpower Planning System," Executive Order 11422, August 15, 1968, Section 1(a), 2(c).
[18] Leach, *American Federalism*, p. 180.

the proliferation of coordinators. With one official responsible for coordinating antipoverty programs, another charged with coordinating urban programs and still another directed to coordinate manpower programs, it is obvious that numerous programs have fallen simultaneously into the jurisdictions of each of these officials.[19]

To complicate matters still further, various federal agencies in the urban field have stimulated the formation and development of counterpart "coordinating structures" at the local level. Thus OEO has had its local partner in Community Action Agencies; HUD has worked through City Demonstration Agencies of the model cities program; and Labor has had both the Cooperative Area Manpower Planning System and Concentrated Employment Program. Each of these local agencies has been charged with "coordinating" a wide range of urban programs, over most of which it has had little effective power.

4. *Upgrading the Quality of Local Personnel*—For years, scholars and federal officials have pointed to the inadequacy of local government personnel as a prime cause of difficulty in federal-local relations.[20] Senator Edmund Muskie, a congressional expert in intergovernmental matters, has declared that local administration is "lacking in quality and experience, unimaginative, and too subject to negative political and bureaucratic pressures."[21]

More professional training is thought to make local administrators better able to learn about and implement federal programs. To this end, there have been numerous proposals and programs for training local personnel in the art of professional management.[22]

Speaking of the need for federal-local cooperation in the area of personnel, former Vice President Humphrey declared, "Our goal must be less friction, less conflict, less duplication, and all within the context of a partnership that is fully collabo-

---

[19] See Sundquist, *Making Federalism Work*, pp. 13ff., for a discussion of the coordination problem in intergovernmental relations.

[20] Leach, *American Federalism*, pp. 183-193, provides a summary of academic and governmental criticisms of the capability of local administrators.

[21] Quoted in Leach, *American Federalism*, p. 186.

[22] Some of these programs are summarized in *ibid.*, pp. 183-192 and Graves, *American Intergovernmental Relations, pp. 952-953.*

rative."[23] Federal policies of (1) increasing communication, (2) encouraging comprehensive planning, (3) creating centers of coordination, and (4) upgrading the quality of local personnel have all been put forward as means of fostering cooperation and lessening conflict in the intergovernmental system. But these solutions, and the diagnosis that lies behind them, do not go to the heart of federal-local conflict.

The Problem Redefined

The above methods of dealing with federal-local friction are based on an assumption that the fundamental problems involved are those of inadequate information and confusion about organizational jurisdiction. Technical methods have been put forward to deal with what have been thought to be technical problems. Organization theorists James D. Thompson and Arthur Tuden have termed such forms of collective decision-making as "computation," and specify that they are appropriate when component organizational units agree both on the causation of a problem and on preferences about possible outcomes of the collective decision.[24] In the case of relations between federal and local organizations (and between separate organizational units *within* each of these groupings), there have been continuing disagreements about both the causes of urban problems and what to do about them. There have been sharp differences of opinion with regard to program goals, procedures, funding levels, and the proper recipients of federal grants. For example, city government leaders have loudly protested the awarding of federal grants to independent local institutions who are openly hostile to City Hall.

If actors and organizations have conflicting policy preferences, then the technical methods of communication, planning, and coordination are unlikely to resolve the differences between them. More discussion and gathering of information might only result in pointing up differences between the organizations. As for coordination, this much-used term is often proposed as a

[23] Humphrey, "A More Perfect Union," quoted in Leach, *American Federalism*, p. 192.

[24] James D. Thompson and Arthur Tuden, "Strategies, Structure, and Processes of Organizational Decision," in *Comparative Studies in Administration*, ed. James D. Thompson (Pittsburgh: University of Pittsburgh Press, 1959), p. 198.

cure for fragmentation, but it does not offer much guidance to one who wishes to make or to understand policy.[25] If organizations disagree about objectives, then coordination may mean that one wins and the other loses. Alternatively, bargaining between them may result in a solution which is somewhere between the opposing preferences. In fortunate circumtances, an integrative solution can make both parties better off than they were. But in no case is coordination among conflicting parties a bloodless and technical process. Certainly, the creation of multiple coordinators and coordinating boards has not eliminated conflict between federal and local agencies.

The differences in perspective between federal and local bodies are due in part to their differing roles as donor and recipient in the grant-in-aid programs. As in foreign aid, a donor's perspective includes a preference for long-term plans, short-term funding, and a number of guidelines regulating how the money may be spent. The recipient's perspective, on the other hand, includes a preference for short-term plans, long-term funding, and relatively few guidelines on spending.

When the problem of conflict has been addressed by designers of intergovernmental structures, it has been treated as a matter of disagreement over goals—to be remedied by collaborative discussion of those goals. Thus, the emphasis has been placed on molding agreement during the formulation of policy, with implementation presumably following in the wake of that initial agreement. This strategy is a perilous one, for, as some recent studies[26] have shown, there are many ways in which initial policy agreement can dissipate during the process of implementation.

If federal-city relations are not characterized by pure cooperation (or by temporary lack of communication between the

[25] Naomi Caiden and Aaron Wildavsky point out that coordination may have various contradictory meanings: efficiency, reliability, coercion, and consent. As a guide for action, they point out, the injunction to "coordinate" is useless. See *Planning and Budgeting in Poor Countries* (New York: John Wiley, 1974), pp. 277-279.

[26] See Martha Derthick, *New Towns In-Town: Why a Federal Program Failed* (Washington, D. C.: The Urban Institute, 1972); and Jeffrey L. Pressman and Aaron Wildavsky, *Implementation: How Great Expectations in Washington Are Dashed in Oakland; Or, Why It's Amazing that Federal Programs Work at All, This Being a Saga of the Economic Development Administration as Told by Two Sympathetic Observers Who Seek to Build Morals on a Foundation of Ruined Hopes* (Berkeley and Los Angeles. University of California Press, 1973).

parties that can be solved by more talking and planning), neither are those relations marked by pure conflict. For the organizations involved have many common interests in operating successful programs and in improving the social and economic health of cities. Thus, federal and city agencies may be seen as engaging in what Schelling calls "mixed motive games," which are combinations of cooperation and conflict.[27] For Schelling, such conflict situations

> are essentially *bargaining* situations. They are situations in which the ability of one participant to gain his ends is dependent to an important degree on the choices or decisions that the other participant will make. The bargaining may be explicit, as when one offers a concession; or it may be by tacit maneuver, as when one occupies or evacuates strategic territory. It may, as in the ordinary haggling of the market-place, take the *status quo* as its zero point and seek arrangements that yield positive gains to both sides; or it may involve threats of damage, including mutual damage, as in a strike, boycott, or price war, or in extortion.[28]

Viewing intergovernmental relations as a bargaining process is useful in keeping us from over-emphasizing either the cooperative or conflictful elements of that behavior. Such a perspective helps us to understand strategic moves made by various players and to suggest policy changes which take into account both shared and divergent values.

Power Asymmetry

A further cause of friction between federal and local agencies is the power asymmetry in the relationship between them. The federal government supplies most of the money for grant-in-aid programs, and it generally insists on a range of guidelines and controls to accompany the financial commitment. A city which desperately needs additional funding is in a poor position to argue about the conditions of a grant. "Cooperative federalism" between relatively wealthy and powerful federal agencies and relatively poor and powerless local agencies is an illusion.

Power asymmetry exacerbates the friction generated by differences in goals and policy preferences. This is not to say

[27] Thomas C. Schelling, *The Strategy of Conflict* (New York: Oxford University Press, 1960), p. 89.
[28] *Ibid.*, p. 5.

that weakness is necessarily a disadvantage in a mixed-motive game. As Schelling notes: "The government that cannot control its balance of payments, or collect taxes, or muster the political unity to defend itself, may enjoy assistance that would be denied it if it could control its own resources."[29] Still, there is no question that city leaders resent their dependence on the federal government and the consequent ability of that government to control so many of their actions.

Mutual Dependence

The federal government's comparative strength does not mean that it can achieve its goals merely by imposing its will on local government agencies. If we follow Dahl's definition of power ("C has power over R to the extent that he can get R to do something that R would not otherwise do"[30]), then we can see that federal and city government agencies have power over each other. For just as cities depend on the federal government for money, so the federal government depends on city agencies to build support for and implement a range of urban programs. Because federal and city governments depend on each other, they can each get the other party to do things that that party would not otherwise do.

John C. Harsanyi has written that, in cases in which A has power over B,

> it very often happens that not only can A exert pressure on B in order to get him to adopt certain specific policies, but B can do the same to A. In particular, B may be able to press A for increased rewards and/or decreased penalties, and for relaxing the standards of compliance required from him and used in administering rewards and penalties to him. Situations of this type we shall call bilateral or reciprocal power situations.[31]

In such situations, both the extent of B's compliant behavior and the incentives that A can provide for B will become matters of bargaining between the two parties. B can exert pressure

[29] *Ibid.*, pp. 22ff.
[30] Robert A. Dahl, "The Concept of Power," *Behavioral Science* 2 (June, 1957), pp. 202-203.
[31] John C. Harsanyi, "Measurement of Social Power, Opportunity Costs, and the Theory of Two-Person Bargaining Games," *Behavioral Science* 7 (January, 1962), p. 74.

on A by withholding his compliance, even though compliance might be more profitable to both parties than noncompliance. B can also exert pressure on A by making the costs of a conflict—including the costs of punishing B for noncompliance —very high.

Even given the supremacy of federal law and the cities' dependence on federal resources, local agencies have a number of bargaining counters. For example, they can threaten to opt out of a federal program; they can threaten a conflict which would be costly for both sides; or they can demonstrate such weakness that emergency federal assistance is made even more likely. Thus, the power imbalance between federal and city governments is not complete; mutual dependence leads to a reciprocal power situation in which bargaining must take place.

The Problem of a Bargaining Arena

For bargaining to take place, the various parties must have some way of transmitting their intentions to each other. As Schelling says, parties to bargaining "must find ways of regulating their behavior, communicating their intentions, letting themselves be led to some meeting of minds, tacit or explicit, to avoid mutual destruction of potential gains."[32] Federal and local officials, with their differing perspectives, career patterns, and associational experiences, sometimes find it difficult to understand each others' policy moves. It has not been easy, therefore, to find effective arenas in which bargaining can proceed. (I will define "arena" as a site at which the exchange of political resources takes place. A list of such resources would include money, authority, information, and physical force, among others.)

Warren Ilchman and Norman Uphoff, whose "political economy" model focuses on exchanges of political resources, speak of such bargaining arenas as "political and administrative infrastructure."[33] They explain that:

---

[32] Schelling, *Strategy of Conflict*, p. 106.
[33] Warren F. Ilchman and Norman Thomas Uphoff, *The Political Economy of Change* (Berkeley and Los Angeles: University of California Press, 1969), pp. 35-37, 208-255.

infrastructure economizes on the use of political resources by increasing *predictability* or *mobility*. The establishment of certain exchange relationships, whether mutually beneficial, legitimated, or coerced, provides for predictability in the amount and kind of resources available to maintain other relationships. When benefits, sanctions, norms, or simply expectations are established with respect to a given pattern of political competition or exercise of authority, compliance may be achieved with the expenditure of fewer resources because political activities and attitudes can be more reliably predicted. Infrastructure contributes to the increased mobility of resources in much the same way that transport systems contribute to greater efficiency of economic production. . . . Infrastructure is used to gain support, enforce authoritative decisions, gather information, deploy coercion, and confer status at less cost than would be the case if established patterns did not exist.[34]

Examples of infrastructure are political parties, interest groups, bureaucracies, and educational systems. Each of these institutions may be seen as an arena which facilitates the exchange of political resources by increasing predictability and mobility in bargaining relationships.

It would be a mistake to assume that the mere creation of an institution for bargaining means that resource exchanges will be more predictable or mobile, or indeed that any bargaining will take place in that institution. We ought to distinguish between *effective* arenas, in which bargains that take place will have some impact on the distribution of resources (such as money, authority, information) among the relevant participants, and *ineffective* or *pseudo-arenas*, in which no real exchanges of resources take place. Bargaining in effective arenas has consequences for outside actors and organizations with whom arena participants may deal; bargaining in pseudo-arenas involves no meaningful changes for the participants and does not have an impact on the outside world.

Although it is true that numerous intergovernmental relations offices, federal-city liaisons, Federal Executive Boards, and interagency regional teams have been created to facilitate "communication" between federal and city officials, they have not served as effective arenas because decisions made in those bodies have not been binding on governmental policy. Without the authority to approve projects and commit funds, such

[34] *Ibid.*, p. 211.

institutions have served as good examples of pseudo-arenas in which agreements that are made do not necessarily have any consequences for the political world outside. Schelling distinguished between "talk" and "moves," saying that "talk is not a substitute for moves. Moves can in some way alter the game, by incurring manifest costs, risks, or a reduced range of subsequent choice; they have an information content, or *evidence* content, of a different character from that of speech."[35] Federal-local communications channels have often stimulated talk, but they have proved frustrating to local leaders who are more interested in moves (decisions as to which group will receive federal money; approval or disapproval of projects; appropriation and delivery of funds). The difficulty in creating effective arenas in which such moves can be made with more reliability and speed has been a continuing problem of intergovernmental relations. Even if goals are agreed upon, projects approved, and funds committed, the need for a bargaining arena does not disappear. For the process of implementation—the carrying out of a policy—requires continuing negotiations and exchanges between relevant governmental actors.

Revenue Sharing and Some Unanswered Questions

It is clear that the creation of communication offices, the stimulation of efforts at comprehensive planning, and the designation of multiple federal and local coordinators (however well trained) will not eradicate the causes of friction between federal and local agencies. Differences in perspective, compounded by power asymmetry and the difficulties of finding effective bargaining arenas, make federal-city relations a thorny policy problem. Because that problem involves organizations with competing objectives, more than computational or technical methods are required to solve it.

But what about federal revenue sharing, which provides funds to cities with relatively few administrative strings attached? This program appears to deal directly with the problem of power asymmetry by reducing (to a modest extent) the imbalance of resources between federal and local governments. And, with the decrease in the number of guidelines, there would

[35] Schelling, *Strategy of Conflict*, p. 117.

seem to be less need for constant intergovernmental bargaining.

Still, the enactment of revenue sharing legislation should not be taken as a panacea for the problems of federal urban programs; a number of important questions remain unanswered. For example, how well equipped are cities to use the additional financial resources? Which organizations or groups within the city are likely to benefit from the shared revenue? What is the impact of outside aid on the possibilities for exercising political leadership at the local level? To answer these questions, we have to know something about the political life of cities which have experienced the infusion of substantial federal programs and the ways in which those programs have affected politics in the city. And, before speculating on the likely effects of changes in federal urban programs, we must gain an understanding of the dynamics of the aid process itself.

The Focus

This study will examine both the interrelationships between federal policy and city politics, and the nature of the continuing interactions between federal and local officials.

Outside aid can have a significant impact on the internal politics of the recipient. As Ilchman has pointed out with reference to foreign aid, "The aid-giver is squarely in the midst of the politics of the recipient country. Every choice he makes affects the distribution of authority, status, and resources in the society—either maintaining the existing distribution or bringing about another."[36] Funds from outside do not come as neutral gifts to a recipient country or city. They result in increasing the comparative resource positions of certain groups while decreasing those of others. And acceptance of those resources often involves costs as well as benefits.

Although federal aid programs can influence local politics, this relationship is not one way. Because the federal donors depend upon local recipients to build support for and implement programs, the final outcome of those programs is determined by local political characteristics as well as federal designs. In focusing both on the effects of federal programs on local politics,

[36] Warren F. Ilchman, "A Political Economy of Foreign Aid: The Case of India," *Asian Survey* 7 (October 1967), p. 670.

and on the influence of local politics on federal programs, I will seek to clarify the nature of the reciprocal power relationships involved in aid programs.

The aid process cannot be fully understood, however, by an analysis of the effects of particular programs. We must also focus on the patterns of continuing, day-to-day interactions between federal and local officials. Such interactions are conditioned both by these officials' images of each other and by their organizational objectives in the aid process itself. In discussing the question of images, I will examine aid officials as individuals in organizations whose members hold certain shared views of the world around them. Such images are useful in dealing with the complex and uncertain environment in which those organizations operate. After exploring the shared perceptions that officials on each side have of their counterparts on the other side, I will point out some of the ways in which these images can influence the nature of the negotiations.

Turning to the subject of organizational motivations, I will use a general model of the aid process to show how intergovernmental actors behave as donors and recipients. I will argue that difficulties result from the inherent constraints of that process and from the competing organizational objectives of the participants.

Having identified sources of recurring friction between donors and recipients, as well as systemic obstacles to the achievement of program goals, I will then evaluate some alternative strategies for dealing with basic problems in the aid process.

The Site

The study will focus on the dynamics of the federal aid process with respect to a particular city—Oakland, California. For a number of reasons, Oakland is a useful site for such a study. First of all, the amount of federal money spent in Oakland has been substantial In 1968, a year in which the city budget totaled $57.9 million, the total nondefense federal spending in Oakland was $95.5 million. If defense expenditures are added, the figure jumps to $487.4 million. Table 2 summarizes federal spending in Oakland for 1968, by department and program.[37] Oakland is also an interesting subject of study because it has been the scene of conscious attempts by federal officials to change the character of local politics. Finally, Oakland has been the focus of federally sponsored administrative experiments which have attempted to overcome obstacles in relations between federal and local officials.

The empirical basis for the study will be drawn to a large extent from my experience in—and observation of—the city of Oakland. From 1967 to 1971 I participated in the Oakland Project, a group of graduate students and faculty members at the University of California, Berkeley, who were engaged in a program of participant-observation in Oakland. As a member of the project, I worked in the office of the mayor from 1967 to 1969. During that time, I concentrated both my

[37] The problems of compiling an inventory of federal funds that enter a city in a given year are enormous. A special Oakland Task Force of the San Francisco Federal Executive Board attempted to carry out such an inventory of Oakland, based on the records of federal departments. But the Task Force reported in 1968 that a "complete and comparable" survey was unattainable for the following reasons: incomplete or inadequate records in regional offices; different data storage and retrieval systems; different reporting periods and methods; varying routing systems; differences in geographical areas by which records are kept; and differences among agencies as to whether cash flow and/or obligations are recorded. (See Oakland Task Force, Federal Executive Board, *An Analysis of Federal Decision-Making and Impact: The Federal Government in Oakland* [San Francisco, 1968; New York: Praeger, 1970], p. 15.)

Although the Task Force did present a partial listing of funds by federal deparments and programs, the Oakland mayor's office was interested in knowing which institutions in the city were receiving funds, how much money was involved, and what projects were being carried out at the local level.

To find the answers to these questions, the mayor's office asked me in 1968 to compile an accounting of federal funding and local recipients in the city. I drew up a questionnaire which requested data on the following items for each program: name of program; federal administering agency; applicable legislation; local administering agency; purpose of program; projects actually carried out; amount of federal grant allocated to Oakland; sharing scale (federal-local); inception date; termination date; plans for renewal. Questionnaires were sent to each federal department, to local agencies which had been listed as recipients of federal funds in a 1966 survey, and to other local institutions which had programs serving the public. Each organization was asked to fill out a questionnaire for every federal program under which it either dispensed or received funds. By including both federal donors and local recipients in the survey, we hoped to increase our ability to discover federal programs in the city and to describe them. The results were published by the city as a *Digest of Current Federal Programs in the City of Oakland*.

The federal-city grant system does not work in a perfectly predictable manner, and funds which are committed do not necessarily arrive when they are executed. For example, money for the Economic Development Administration's program had been committed by the agency for Port of Oakland projects. But because of a host of disagreements and delays, the expected funds did not arrive in 1968. Thus, the figure for the Commerce Department represents a commitment which did not in fact materialize during that year.

Table 2: Federal Expenditures in Oakland Totaled Over $95 Million
in 1968, Excluding Defense

Federal Agency and Program	Dollar Amount of Grant
Department of Health, Education, and Welfare	
Compensatory Education .... $	2,182,844
Public Assistance	19,472,154
Vocational Education	229,289
Other (Libraries, Health)	2,604,177
TOTAL	24,488,464
Department of Commerce	
Economic Development Administration	8,275,780
TOTAL	8,275,780
Department of Housing and Urban Development	
Urban Renewal	6,635,115
Public Housing	1,522,995
Other (Mass Transit, Recreation, Planning, Water and Sewer Grant)	5,332,656
TOTAL	13,490,766
Department of Labor	
Concentrated Employment Program	3,486,670
East Bay Skills Center	3,500,000
Neighborhood Youth Corps	166,930
TOTAL	7,153,600
Office of Economic Opportunity	
Community Action Program	1,723,728
VISTA	121,797
College Work-Study	265,597
Inner-City Project	352,354
TOTAL	2,463,476
Department of Agriculture	
School Lunches, Research, Commodity Distribution...	5,580,136
TOTAL	5,580,136
Post Office Department	
Employee Salaries	24,000,000
Other (Rent, Maintenance, Supplies)	718,000
TOTAL	24,718,000
Department of Transportation: TOTAL (Highways)...	9,289,150
TOTAL NONDEFENSE	95,459,372
TOTAL DEFENSE (Military and Civilian Payroll; Prime Contract Awards to Contractors in Oakland)........	391,897,000
GRAND TOTAL	$487,356,372

Source: *Digest of Current Federal Programs in the City of Oakland.* Prepared for
Mayor John H. Reading by Jeffrey L. Pressman, October 1, 1968.

work and my observation on relations between federal and city agencies. To supplement this observation, in the summer of 1970 I conducted lengthy open-ended interviews in Washington with 21 federal officials who have been involved in administering federal programs related to Oakland. And in the summer of 1972, in order to examine the perceptions that federal and local officials had of each other, I interviewed twelve federal officials with responsibility for programs in Oakland and eleven Oakland city officials who were charged with negotiating with federal agencies.

To outline briefly the coming chapters:

Chapter 2 will examine Oakland's governmental and political system, concentrating on those persons and institutions with whom federal officials have most often dealt.

Chapter 3 will focus on the experience of a series of federal programs which precipitated change in the local political system and conflict between federal and local officials. These programs made possible the creation, with federal funds, of a new arena for political action by representatives of the poor. I will show how the occupants of this new arena became engaged in heated disputes with those in the city's electoral arena, and I will discuss the ways in which the arenas differed from each other. In studying the creation of this new arena, I will demonstrate both the effect of federal policy on local politics and the effect of local politics on policy outcomes. For, although the federal programs did alter political relationships within the city, the results of those programs were strongly influenced by the patterns of behavior identified in chapter 2.

Moving from an analysis of particular programs to a focus on the continuing interactions between aid participants, chapter 4 examines the perceptions that federal and local officials have of each other and explores the implications of those perceptions for negotiations between the officials.

Chapter 5 presents a general model of the aid process to show how difficulties result from inherent constraints of that process and from the conflicting organizational objectives of donors and recipients.

Chapter 6 uses observations from previous chapters, and the experience of recent intergovernmental innovations, to suggest directions for future policy in federal-city relations.

2
The Receptacle: Oakland's Political System[*]

Before examining the impact of federal programs on Oakland's political system, it is first necessary to look closely at that system itself—governmental structures, organized groups, and patterns of political activity. As stated earlier, I will concentrate on those local actors with whom federal officials most frequently dealt.

The recipients of federal dollars in Oakland have been numerous—including postal employees, military personnel, and many other people in a variety of occupations and institutions. But few local individuals have been visible to federal agencies and have been of concern to those federal officials who have consciously sought to stimulate political changes in the city. For a number of reasons, I will be particularly concerned with the role of the mayor. The Oakland City Charter states that it is the responsibility of the mayor to "represent the city in intergovernmental relations as directed by the Council."[1] In fact, as we shall see, the city council and city manager have not shown much inclination to become involved in federal

* Much of the analysis found in this chapter was initially developed in my article, "Preconditions of Mayoral Leadership," in *The American Political Science Review* 66 (June 1972), pp. 511-524.
[1] *Oakland City Charter* Section 219.

urban programs; they have left the mayor with most of the
task of handling federal-city contacts. Intergovernmental relations do not merely consist of governmental structures in-
teracting with each other; the men and women representing
various governmental units strongly influence the pattern of
those relations. And in Oakland, it has been the mayor who
has spoken for city hall in its relationship with outside organizations.

Federal aid might be considered as a way of providing help
for mayors who do not have sufficient resources to cope with
the problems facing their cities. And political scientists have
described a model of the successful political leader who can
"pyramid" limited initial resources into substantial political
capital. Robert Dahl has written that:

> Although the kinds and amounts of resources available to political man
> are always limited and at any given moment fixed, they are not . .
> permanently fixed as to either kind or amount. Political man can
> use his resources to gain influence, and he can then use his influence
> to gain more resources. Political resources can be pyramided in much
> the same way that a man who starts out in business sometimes pyramids
> a small investment into a large corporate empire.[2]

Dahl shows how Mayor Richard C. Lee of New Haven was
able to use federal redevelopment funds to enlarge his base
of power both inside and outside of the city administration
by building his staff, carrying out politically popular projects,
and then converting popular support for those projects into
acquiescence in an "executive-centered coalition" with himself
at the center.[3]

A local political actor's ability to pyramid federal resources
in this manner is by no means assured, however. Opportunities

[2] Robert A. Dahl, *Who Governs?* (New Haven: Yale University Press, 1961), p. 227.
For further discussion of political entrepreneurship and the pyramiding of resources,
see Edward C. Banfield, *Political Influence* (New York: The Free Press, 1961), ch.
8 and pp. 17, 309, 312-313, 320-321; Aaron Wildavsky, *Leadership in a Small Town*
(Totowa, N. J.: Bedminster Press, 1964), pp. 244-245, 248; H. H. Gerth and C. Wright
Mills, *From Max Weber* (New York: Oxford University Press, 1946), p. 109; Andrew
S. McFarland, *Power and Leadership in Pluralist Systems* (Stanford, Calif.: Stanford
University Press, 1969), pp. 153-219; Alexander L. George, "Political Leadership and
Social Change in American Cities," *Daedalus* 97 (Fall 1968), p. 1197.

[3] See Dahl, *Who Governs?* pp. 115-140, 200-203. Raymond E. Wolfinger, in *The Politics
of Progress* (Englewood Cliffs, N. J.: Prentice-Hall, 1974), provides a detailed analysis
of Lee's use of federal resources.

24 Federal Programs and City Politics

for such activity may be limited by the political structure of a city (electoral system, parties, groups) and by governmental structure. Furthermore, the ability to expand a resource base— which is a critical part of the ability to exercise leadership[4]—may be strongly influenced by the personality of the actor himself. Although social forces and governmental structures set limits to what *any* person might be able to do with added federal resources in a particular city, personal variability should not be discounted.[5]

This chapter will deal with the political and governmental structure of Oakland, with a particular focus on Mayor John H. Reading, the man who has represented the city government in its relations with federal agencies. By comparing Mayor Reading's use of political resources with that of his predecessor, we can assess the difference that personality makes in mayoral leadership. But that leadership is conditioned by the political and governmental systems, and I will emphasize the links between Oakland's political system and the forms that mayoral leadership can take.

When assessing political leadership in cities, it is useful to keep in mind a model of such leadership which emerges from the literature of social science and the recommendations of national commissions on urban problems. The mayor is usually selected as the prime candidate for urban democratic leader-

[4] Andrew McFarland defines leadership in the following way: "A *leader* may be defined as one who has unusual *influence*. Influence may be viewed as one's capacity to make people behave differently than they would have otherwise. A leader may also be defined as one who has unusual *power*. Here we view 'power' as a person's capacity to make others do something that they would not do otherwise and that the person specifically wants or intends." McFarland, *Power and Leadership*, p. 154. In structures of dispersed, decentralized power, successful leaders are those who can pyramid resources to supplement their limited formal authority and thus gain influence over the behavior of others.

[5] Discussing the impact of personality on politics, Fred I. Greenstein has stated that the likelihood of personal impact: (1) increases to the degree that the environment admits of restructuring; (2) varies with the actor's location in the environment; and (3) varies with the personal strengths and weaknesses of the actor. For Greenstein, personal variability is most likely to manifest itself in "ambiguous situations" in which "political actors lack mental sets which might lead them to structure their perceptions and resolve ambiguities." See Greenstein, "The Impact of Personality on Politics: An Attempt to Clear Away Underbrush," *The American Political Science Review* 61 (September 1967), p. 638. McFarland also notes the importance of an ambiguous environment in providing opportunities for personal initiative; he views leadership opportunities in "conflicting expectations among others about the person's behavior in a position." McFarland *Power and Leadership*, p. 203.

ship, and his task is a difficult one. The leader is advised to devote his energies and direct his constituency toward the following urban goals: effective and humane law enforcement; redevelopment linked to speedy relocation in decent housing of those displaced by redevelopment; expansion of a city's financial resources by increasing taxes or by attracting new industry; improvement of educational quality and relationships between the schools and community; construction of low-cost public housing; generation of new jobs; and creation of training and job placement programs. Besides these substantive goals, the urban leader would strive to maintain within the political system a process of constructive dialogue between diverse groups which would contribute to harmony in the system.

In pursuing these goals suggested by writers on urban problems, a mayor who wants to be an effective urban leader would have to exercise control and direction over the city council and relevant city departments: such as, schools, redevelopment, housing, and police. The successful leader would attempt to stretch his legal jurisdiction as far as possible. Furthermore, he would have to activate nongovernmental groups in the community to support his tasks by promising rewards and threatening sanctions. He would have to persuade businessmen to locate factories in his city, to initiate job-training programs, and to develop jobs. He would have to persuade labor unions to open places in apprenticeship programs to minority groups. And he would have to persuade black community groups that he was carrying out programs that would benefit them and which deserved their support.

An ideal urban leader would use his control of the mechanism of a political party to further his policy preferences, by supporting the nomination and election of candidates who were willing to support him. Furthermore, a model leader would be willing to use publicity in order to appeal to the public to back him against opponents by voting in elections or by trying to influence recalcitrant groups.

In order to exercise leadership over these various groups—to make them do what they would otherwise not do—the mayor-as-leader who emerges from the literature would require various initial resources. They include:

(a) sufficient financial and staff resources on the part of the city government;

(b) city jurisdiction in social program areas such as education, housing, redevelopment, and job training;

(c) the mayor's jurisdiction within the government in those fields;

(d) a salary that would permit him to spend full time at his job;

(e) sufficient staff support for policy planning, speech writing intergovernmental relations, and political work;

(f) ready vehicles for publicity, such as friendly newspapers or television stations;

(g) politically oriented groups—including a political party—that the mayor can mobilize to help him achieve particular goals.

Because most mayors lack extensive formal authority, proponents of mayoral leadership have rarely concerned themselves with the problems posed by unrestrained exercise of that leadership. The system's capacity to restrain leadership may be seen as a function of the mayor's dependence upon other independent groups and of the degree to which elections can pose a competitive challenge to the mayor.

Such a model will provide a guide in this chapter for assessing the opportunities that Oakland's political system provides for leadership and resource-pyramiding.

In subsequent chapters some of the effects of outside aid on political leadership (and the effects of local leadership on federal programs) will be discussed. But we must first examine the foundations of that leadership in the local community itself.

ENVIRONMENT

The City

In 1966, when the University of California's Survey Research Center carried out a "701" Household Survey of Poverty in

Oakland,[6] the total household population of the city was 365,490. The racial composition of the city is summarized in Table 3.

Table 3: Racial Composition of Oakland, California (1966)

Ethnicity	Number	Percent
Total Persons	365,490	100
White (excluding Spanish surname)	201,180	55
White (with Spanish surname)	35,200	10
Negro	110,050	30
Other Non-White	19,060	5

Source: Survey Research Center, University of California, *Poverty and Poverty Programs in Oakland*. (Berkeley, 1967), p. 26.

Among people defined as below the "poverty level"—earning below $2,500 per year for a single individual and below $4,000 for a family of four—minority groups (black people and Mexican-Americans) were over-represented. Whereas black people made up 30 percent of the city's total population, they constituted 45 percent of the poverty population. Mexican-Americans, who made up 10 percent of the city's population, were 14 percent of the poverty population.

One of the most discouraging statistics concerning Oakland has been the city's unemployment rate. Table 4 compares the Oakland and national unemployment figures. Among blacks and Mexican-Americans, the unemployment rate was found to be 12 percent, as opposed to 5 percent among whites and 8 percent among "orientals and other non-whites."[7] In the Oakland hills, unemployment was 3.9 percent; in the West and East Oakland ghettoes, the figures were 14.3 percent and 14.4 percent, respectively.[8]

Oakland, then, is the kind of city that has been discussed at length in the news media as an example of the "urban crisis." It is characterized by an increasingly large minority population, geographical separation and emotional tension between races, and a high unemployment rate.

[6] Section 701 of the Federal Housing Act of 1954, as amended, provides funds for urban planning assistance.

[7] Stanford Research Institute report, p. 12.

[8] *Ibid.*, p. 16.

Table 4: Oakland's Unemployment Rate is Significantly Higher
Than the National Average

Rates	Percent of Civilian Labor Force Unemployed	
*Crude Rates**	*Oakland*	*United States*
Total (all civilian workers)	8.4	4.1
Males, 20 years and over	4.8	2.3
Females, 20 years and over	8.3	3.9
Both sexes, 14 to 19 years	30.5	13.0
*Seasonally Adjusted Rates***		
Total (all civilian workers)	7.7	4.0
Males, 20 years and over	4.6	2.5
Females, 20 years and over	7.5	3.9
Both sexes, 14 to 19 years	26.7	12.4

Source: Stanford Research Institute, *Human Resources Development for Oakland: Problems and Policies* (Menlo Park, 1968), p. 10.

* For Oakland, the simple unemployment rate based on all cases included in the 701 survey. For the United States, the mean adjusted unemployment rate for May, June, July, and August.

** Mean seasonally adjusted rate for May, June, July, and August. For Oakland, an approximate seasonal adjustment was made for interviews completed in each month, based on U.S. seasonal adjustment figures.

Political Environment: The Non-Politics of Oakland

It often appears as though politics in Oakland does not exist. In 1969, when elections were held for mayor, city council, and the board of education, the candidate response was tepid at best. Two little-known men emerged to challenge Mayor Reading's attempt for reelection; two new candidates filed against two of the three incumbents on the school board; and all three city councilmen who were up for reelection were unopposed.

In a city marked by serious divisions, what causes the avoidance of electoral politics? Many answers have been suggested: the lack of resources and power in city government; the middle and upper class white bias of the at-large election system, which makes candidacies expensive and extraordinarily difficult; the city council's action in raising filing fees from $20 to $200; the paltry salaries of elected officials.

A further reason for the anemic condition of Oakland's electoral process has been the noticeable absence of political party activity in municipal elections. This absence has, no doubt, been encouraged by the nonpartisan nature of the municipal ballot, which gives voters no indication of the party to which a candidate belongs. But formal nonpartisanship is not a sufficient explanation for party inaction. In neighboring Berkeley, for example, a liberal Democratic caucus organized in the 1950s managed to win substantial majorities on both the city council and school board. Slates of candidates were endorsed and "Democratic Newsletters" were distributed—although the form of the ballot remained officially nonpartisan. In formally "nonpartisan" San Francisco, Democratic and Republican organizations have also been active.

If the form of the ballot is not an adequate explanation for the lack of party activity in Oakland, what factors can be identified upon which to base such an explanation? One factor is that party leaders in Oakland—who *are* active in national, state, and even county campaigns—seem to share the lack of interest exhibited by Oakland citizens (in 1969 Oakland Project interviews) in their city. They argue that opportunities for success are small and that citizen indifference toward city affairs makes city government in Oakland unattractive to ambitious politicians.

Another cause of party inactivity in Oakland has been the lack of organized politically interested groups in the city upon which a party or mayor could build. When the Associated Students Union of Oakland (an organization of liberal student activists) tried to form a "coalition" in 1968 and 1969 to work for changes in school procedure and curriculum, they found—as one leader put it—"that there was no one to coalesce with." Labor has not played a significant role in city politics since the 1940s. And business groups, though formally endorsing certain nonpartisan causes like charter reform, have not heavily involved themselves in city politics. In Berkeley, university groups, PTAs, and civic organizations combined to form the Democratic caucus. Oakland does not have these kinds of groups upon which to build a party, and the party organizations themselves are less than healthy groups.

Whatever the reasons, it is clear that the electoral arena has not been the scene of the "action" in contemporary Oakland. (The mayoral campaign of Black Panther leader Bobby Seale did stimulate considerable electoral activity in 1973, but it is not clear that the enthusiasm generated by that campaign will lead to a continuing commitment to black electoral organization in Oakland.)

The absence of active parties and groups—and of city-wide politics itself—constitutes a grave limitation on local political leadership. If they existed, such groups might give a mayor the opportunity to identify interests which had become aggregated by and articulated through organizations. Furthermore, groups and parties could perform the function of recruiting political leaders with whom the mayor could bargain. Finally, the mayor could use friendly groups as vehicles for political education in the goals toward which he was working and as organizing devices to bring citizens together in support of these goals. In a political environment without such groups and parties, leadership is difficult.

Form of Government: The Limits of City Hall Control

Before discussing Oakland city government, it is well to understand the jurisdictional limits of that government. For only a few of the problem areas that have been usually associated with the "urban crisis" are directly under the control of Oakland's city council and city manager. The school system, for example, is completely independent of City Hall, except for the provision that the city council may pass a 5 percent "emergency tax" for the schools. Another powerful independent body is the Oakland Board of Port Commissioners, which was established in 1927 as an independent department of the city with exclusive control over management of the Port of Oakland.

Although redevelopment and housing have been two of the most controversial policy areas in Oakland, the commissions that have jurisdiction in these areas are also "autonomous." The Oakland Redevelopment Agency and the Oakland Housing Authority, funded by the federal government, have the power to hire and fire their own employees. Finally, the local poverty agency, the Oakland Economic Development Council, Inc., was independent from City Hall from 1967 to 1971. This agency, which operated important manpower programs and community action projects, received over $5.2 million from the federal government in 1968.

Now that we have considered some of those governmental bodies in the city's environment which are outside City Hall, let us look more closely at the inside of city government itself.

The Separation of Politics from Administration

In a seminal article which appeared in 1887, Woodrow Wilson declared that "administration lies outside the proper sphere of *politics*. Administrative questions are not political questions. Although politics sets the tasks for administration, it should not be suffered to manipulate its offices."[9] Political actors should meet to fashion a broad policy which will serve as a clear directive for subsequent action. But once those guidelines are established, the task of policy making for the politician is ended. Now the problem is one of technical efficiency in carrying out the policy, and only a scientifically trained administrator is able to perform this task competently.

This separation of politics from administration, a hallmark of the Progressive era in American politics, lies at the root of the council-manager form of government. In Oakland, according to the city charter: "The Council shall be the governing body of the City. It shall exercise the corporate powers of the City and ... it shall be vested with all powers of legislation." However, the charter goes on to state that the council "shall have no administrative powers."[10]

The mayor, who is a member of the city council, occupies a special place in the "political" side of Oakland city government. As described by the city charter, his duties sound impressive:

The Mayor shall be the chief elective officer of the City, responsible for providing leadership and taking issues to the people and marshalling public interest in and support for municipal activity. He shall recommend to the Council such legislation as he deems necessary and shall encourage programs for the physical, economic, social and cultural development of the City. He shall preside over meetings of the Council, shall be the ceremonial head of the City, and shall represent the City in intergovernmental relations as directed by the Council.[11]

[9] Woodrow Wilson, "The Study of Administration," reprinted in *Political Science Quarterly* 56 (December 1941), p. 494.
[10] *Oakland City Charter*, Section 207.
[11] *Ibid.*, Section 219.

Once again, the line is clearly drawn between politics and administration: "The Mayor shall have no administrative authority, it being the intent of this Charter that the Mayor shall provide community leadership, while administrative responsibilities are assigned to the City Manager."

Thus, according to the charter, the mayor is to lead public opinion, the council is to formulate policy, and the city manager is to administer the policy. The manager has the power "to execute and enforce all laws and ordinances and policies of the Council and to administer the affairs of the City."[12] Under the city manager's jurisdiction is the preparation and submission of the city budget and the administration of the city government's departments.

In theory, the council sets policy and the manager carries it out. However, in practice, the relationship between politics and administration in Oakland has been strongly affected by the personalities of the people holding city offices and by the wide disparity in the levels of resources available to the politicians on one hand and the administrators on the other.

An examination of comparative resources helps to explain why there is a strong tendency in Oakland for administration to devour politics, for the mayor and council to follow the manager's lead in the policy making process. First of all, the mayor and councilmen are not intended to serve full time at their jobs; the city manager, on the other hand, is enjoined by the charter "to devote his entire time to the duties and interests of the City."[13] Salary levels underscore this difference: as of 1973, the mayor earned only $7,500 and each councilman earned $3,600 per year, but the city manager's annual salary was $38,940. It would be a rare councilman or mayor who could afford to spend full time on his job.

This imbalance between the political and administrative sides of Oakland city government is further increased by a disparity in the staff and informational resources available to the council and manager. For the entire city council is served by just one secretary, who answers the phone, arranges appointments, types letters, and administers the Christmas program of the Municipal Employees' Choir. The mayor is not

[12] *Ibid.*, Section 404.
[13] *Ibid.*

much better off, with one administrative assistant and three secretaries.

The city manager, in contrast, may utilize the manpower and informational resources of all city departments under his control. Furthermore, the manager has three full-time staff assistants in his own office who help him keep abreast of departmental communications. The finance and budget directors, who serve under the city manager, provide him with information regarding the allocation and utilization of city funds by the departments. As a result, the city manager tends to know more than anyone else about city government structures, processes, and substantive policies.

How Typical Are Oakland's Governmental Structures and Political Rules for Cities of Its Size?

According to data in *The Municipal Year Book* for 1968,[14] the council-manager form of government is the most prevalent form for cities in the 250,000 to 500,000 population range.

Table 5: Form of Government for Cities of 250,000–500,000 Population

Number of Cities Reporting	Mayor-Council	Council-Manager	Commission
27	11	13 (including Oakland)	3

For the twenty-seven cities above 500,000 population, the pattern was quite different. Twenty-two had the mayor-council form, while only five were council-manager.

Of the thirteen cities in the 250,000 to 500,000 group which had a council-manager form, six (including Oakland) had a mayor directly elected by the people. In six other cities, the council selected a mayor from among its own members. And in the remaining city, the mayoral selection process was classified as "other."[15]

As to ballot affiliation for general city elections, data was presented for twenty-five cities in the relevant population

[14] *The Municipal Year Book* (Washington: International City Managers' Association, 1968), p. 54.
[15] *Ibid.*, p. 55.

group. In six of these cities, a national party affiliation appeared on the local ballot; in nineteen cities (including Oakland) such affiliation did not appear.[16]

Data regarding the methods of councilmanic nomination and election for twenty-six cities in this population range are summarized in Table 6. Most cities in this group had at-large nominations *and* elections of councilmen. Oakland was the only city to have "nomination by wards and at large, elect at large." Seven of the nine Oakland councilmen are elected for specific districts; one is elected at large. (The mayor is also elected at large.) But all candidates are voted upon by the entire city. Thus the same city-wide majority can enforce its preference in each district.

Table 6: Combinations of Nomination and Election of Councilmen in Cities of 250,000–500,000

Number of Cities Reporting	Nominate at Large Elect at Large	Nominate by Wards Elect at Large	Nominate by Wards Elect by Wards
26	15	3	2

Nominate by Wards and at Large Elect at Large	Nominate by Wards and at Large Elect by Wards and at Large
1 (Oakland)	5

Source: The Municipal Year Book (Washington: International City Manager's Association, 1968), p. 59.

Although its nomination-election system is somewhat unique, Oakland's council-manager form of government and nonpartisan ballot represent practices that are popular among cities in the 250,000 to 500,000 group.

Jerome Keithley: The Triumph of Administration[17]

We have seen that the position of city manager is blessed with certain structural advantages. But a potential monopoly on staff and informational resources is not the only reason for city manager domination of the Oakland governmental process

[16] *Ibid.*, p. 58.
[17] I am indebted to Arnold Meltsner for insights into the city manager's methods of operation.

in recent years; for Jerome Keithley, who served as city manager from 1966 to 1972, was a man who was adept at dealing with the internal environment of city government. The city council's power to fire the city manager gives councilmen an ultimate trump card to play against the manager, but Keithley's performance in his job gained him the solid and enthusiastic support of the council, and the reasons for this support were numerous.

First of all, Keithley shared the views of most councilmen as to what the goals of city administration should be: efficiency, cost-cutting, and thus lower taxes. Second, City Manager Keithley used his access to departmental records to satisfy as quickly as possible councilmen's requests for information. For example, a few years ago, citizens complained to the mayor that the utilities tax was bearing most heavily on old people. The council requested Keithley to look into the matter, and a city budget analyst immediately began carrying out a study.

A further way in which Keithley built council support was his practice of letting the councilmen make decisions in areas in which they were particularly interested. For example, the city manager allowed the council to have jurisdiction over the budget for "civic organizations"—such as the Chamber of Commerce, the Elks Club, the Italian-American Federation, and the California Spring Garden and Home Show Committee. In 1969, this budget of "plums" amounted to $319,999.

Finally, Keithley built support on the council by being "one of the guys." He was a regular attender at city council dinners and at ball games at the Coliseum, events that the mayor often avoids. Thus, the manager used personal friendship—as well as access to valuable resources and shared value orientations—to maintain city council support.

What was the social and political outlook of this man who managed to create such a secure position for himself in Oakland's governmental system? Basically, Keithley did not see his role of manager as political. He took the charter literally, and he was concerned primarily with the physically oriented departments that were under this formal jurisdiction. Within his area of control, Keithley was devoted to efficiency—which to him meant cost-cutting, the avoidance of duplication, and the provision of better service.

For Keithley, the federal government was a source of frustration. Although the city needed federal money, it sometimes seemed to him that it was not worth the trouble it took to get these funds. The money never appeared to come on time, and lack of communication between federal auditors and operators meant that it was difficult to keep books efficiently. Furthermore, the city manager resented what he considered undue federal pressure—for instance, when the Department of Housing and Urban Development asked him not to fire two building inspectors, or face rejection of the city's "workable program" for federal redevelopment funds.

Armed with his considerable advantages, the city manager defined "policy" and "administration" in a manner in which "administration" loomed very large and "policy" very small. When the mayor complained in July 1968 that the police chief's stringent restrictions on policemen's use of guns (a decision in which the city manager had concurred but about which the mayor had never been consulted) constituted a dangerous policy decision which should be overturned by the council, the city manager disagreed. The manager's reasoning was clear: "A policy decision would be that policemen in Oakland should carry guns. Administrative decisions would be when they should carry guns, where they should carry guns, and how they should use those guns."

The City Attorney

The city manager's definition of "policy" and "administration" has usually been supported by the city attorney, Edward Goggin, who is appointed by the council but who takes his lead from the city manager.[18] Goggin has a penchant for defining the area of permissible action by the city government as extremely narrow; within the government, Goggin tends to rule against expanded city council jurisdiction. For example, when Mayor Reading set up a Council Human Relations Committee to hear citizens' grievances, Goggin ruled that the committee

[18] For a fascinating description of the crucial role in policy making that can be played by a city attorney, see "The Cambridge City Manager" in *Public Administration and Policy Development: A Case Book*, ed. Harold Stein (New York: Harcourt Brace, 1952).

could take no action that was not approved by the city administration. Embodying numerous restrictive interpretation, the city attorney's opinions constitute another obstacle with which the mayor must contend.

The City Council

Elected officials in Oakland are faced with a constraining governmental structure and a scarcity of resources both within and outside of City Hall. The mayor, a member of the council with just one vote out of nine, is not in an awesome position himself. But a determined majority of the council *could* direct the city manager and attorney to follow its leadership—or it could fire the manager and hire a new one who would work toward its goals.

Process of Entry.—Of the present members of the council, five were originally appointed and four were originally elected. According to a study made by a civic reform group, the Oakland Citizens for a Responsive Government, "appointment politics" has been a tradition in Oakland. Table 7 summarizes the results of that study.

Table 7: Appointment Politics Has Been Common in Oakland, 1953–1968

Office	Number of Changes	Originally Appointed	Originally Elected
Mayor	2	1	1
Councilmen	17	9	8

Source: Oakland Citizens for Responsive Government, "Effect of Appointments Upon the Oakland Governmental Structure." *Newsletter*, June 1969.

Once on the council, incumbents tend to be able to survive subsequent elections with ease. No "appointed incumbent" has lost the ensuing election in the past sixteen years. Overall, in the period between the spring elections of 1953 through the spring elections of 1969, only a handful of incumbents have lost. Table 8 shows the enviable electoral record of Oakland incumbents. As we have seen, elections to the city council are run on a city-wide basis, although a candidate for council must live in the district he wishes to represent.

Table 8:   Incumbents Have Been Successful in Oakland Politics 1953–1969

Office	Number of Incumbents' Campaigns	Number of Incumbents' Victories	Number of Incumbents' Defeats
Mayor	6	5	1
Councilmen	34	29*	5

Source: Oakland Citizens for Responsive Government.
* Twelve of these were unopposed.

Process of Business.—Inside the council, there are two standing committees: Ways and Means, which considers tax and
budget questions; and Civic Action, with a vague jurisdiction
in the area of human relations. Whenever the councilmen
engage in semi-intensive study, it is usually done through one
of these committees.

Official city council meetings take place at 7:30 p.m. on
Tuesdays and at 10:30 a.m. on Thursdays, but most decisions
are made at special "work sessions" before the council meetings—in the mayor's office on Thursdays and over dinner on
Tuesday evenings. Although citizens' groups and the press have
raised pointed questions about the secrecy of such meetings,
both mayor and council have felt that they can be more honest
with each other at such sessions, and also be shielded from
pressure.

Social and Political Attitudes of the Council.—Although
liberals have occasionally been elected to the council, the social
and political attitudes of most councilmen tend to be conservative; these men are distrustful of government action in social
areas and disturbed by the growing consciousness and militancy
of black people. They feel that the main part of the poverty
problem is the motivation of poor people themselves. To one
councilman, for example, the employment situation is a result
of the workings of human nature: "Some ethnic groups just
don't want to work, so there really isn't much use in training
them."[19]

At times, the council seems to pretend that Oakland's problems do not exist. In July 1968, the Coordinating Community
Council (made up of sixteen school-community councils) asked
the city council to levy a five-cent "emergency" tax to lease

[19] Interview, August 24, 1967.

portable classrooms and purchase land, if needed, so that nineteen elementary schools in Oakland could eliminate double sessions. The chairman of the Ways and Means Committee admitted that the city council had the right to levy the tax, but he noted that "what constitutes an emergency is a matter of opinion." He pointed out that, historically, an emergency in the schools had meant a "fire or a catastrophe." Overcrowding and double sessions were not in that category, and the council did not accede to the request.[20]

The mayor has consistently tried to get the council to take a greater interest in federal programs, but city council unwillingness to face up to the existence of urban problems has posed a significant obstacle to these mayoral initiatives. In April 1969, Mayor Reading called the council together in a "work session" to discuss an "affirmative action policy" on employment, which was needed to qualify the city for federal funds from the Department of Commerce's Economic Development Administration. The mayor felt that the city should pledge to employ— and encourage others to employ—blacks and Mexican Americans who were in need of jobs. Reading was emphatic: "There's no question about it: Negroes and Mexican-Americans have double the unemployent rate of whites. If we are not willing to go along with this we're wasting our time talking to EDA."

The councilmen, however, were not so sure; it was not right, they thought, to single out Negroes and Mexican-Americans for special mention. "Are we closing the door here?" asked one conservative. "We can't discriminate against anyone." Sadly, the mayor gave in and told the council to strike the phrase "Negroes and Mexican-Americans" from the document; the word "minorities" would be substituted. "But for the record," the mayor remarked, "I think it should be included. The basic reason I think it should be included is because it's right." Still, the council had won: no groups were specifically mentioned in the document.[21] Once again, the Oakland City Council had managed to avoid mentioning an unpleasant problem. And the mayor had failed to interest other city actors in a federal social program.

[20] *The Montclarion*, July 24, 1968.
[21] *The Montclarion*, April 16, 1969.

Responses to Conflict: The "Retrenchment" or "Shrinking Violet Syndrome"

If there is one thing that Oakland city councilmen do not like, it is conflict. For example, an easy going councilman mentioned controversy as the one drawback of life on the council.[22] Another once argued at a Charter Revision Committee meeting that the mayor ought to have the power to suspend the taking effect of ordinances temporarily, thus allowing the council to change its mind away from the glare of publicity and public pressure.

The process of conflict avoidance is discussed in the literature of organization theory. Anthony Downs describes the "shrinking violet syndrome" in which a bureau avoids conflict by narrowing its actions and affecting fewer external agents.[23] Matthew Holden, Jr., in an article on " 'Imperialism' in Bureaucracy," states that:

> Perhaps the most neglected cases are those in which there is a clear disposition toward retrenchment or self-limitation. It is not merely that the agency adopts kid-glove tactics in order to maintain a cooperative relationship with a constituency, but that it actually denies its powers.[24]

In order to avoid the conflict, uncertainty, and turbulence of a hostile urban environment, the Oakland City Council goes beyond merely narrowing its actions and denying its powers. Indeed, the council follows a consistent policy of actively giving up jurisdiction in areas that are considered troublesome. Problems are "farmed out" to other groups and to other levels of government.

When a council Human Relations Committee was attacked by a critical councilman in late 1967 as a "secret ombudsman," the city council decided to deal with Oakland's administrative grievance problem in another way. For the low price of $10,000, the city was able to enter into an agreement with Alameda County whereby the (powerless) County Human Relations Commission would add another member to its staff, with that

---

[22] Interview, August 24, 1967.
[23] Anthony Downs, *Inside Bureaucracy* (Boston: Little, Brown, 1967), p. 217.
[24] Matthew Holden, Jr., " 'Imperialism' in Bureaucracy," *The American Political Science Review* 60 (December 1966), p. 945.

individual concentrating his efforts on Oakland. The city government was out of the human relations business, the restrictions on the county commission's activity made it unlikely that
any administrator would be embarrassed or threatened; and
the cost to the city was only $10,000.

Experience with federal programs has provided numerous
examples of council retrenchment and jurisdiction disposal.
When Mayor Reading suggested to the council that it might
consider taking over the local poverty program under the 1967
Green Amendment, there was little enthusiasm for such a
move—quite apart from the city attorney's dire legal warnings.
A cautious councilman even proposed that the entire problem
be given up to the state.[25]

Avoidance of conflict should not be confused with passivity
or openness to mayoral leadership. For some mayor initiatives—for example, a move for more control of federally funded
social programs—would mean more responsibility, more conflict, and more hostility for the council members. Besides, the
council tends to be resentful of any independent status enjoyed
by the mayor. Thus, the council's Ways and Means Committee
recommended in 1968 that the mayor's Manpower Commission
be cut from the city budget.

Even the mayor's own office in City Hall is not necessarily
friendly terrain. One of Mayor Reading's original secretaries,
who was in charge of greeting visitors to the office, had voiced
her strong disapproval of the mayor's quiet style and of his
"too liberal" policies relating to minorities. Therefore, in the
fall of 1967, the mayor decided to transfer this disloyal secretary
to another department. But the city manager's office advised
caution in taking this step, and civil service moved slowly in
arranging a transfer. Meanwhile, councilmen complained that
they disapproved of the change. It was not until the spring
of 1969—a year and a half later—that the city manager and
civil service told the mayor that the secretary could be trans-
ferred. This incident illustrates both the councilmen's resentment of independent mayoral moves and the lack of staff
resources and freedom in the mayor's office.

The city council avoids federal programs because a number

[25] *Oakland Tribune*, May 29, 1968.

of the councilmen are opposed to ambitious social projects and because the council in general has a strong distaste for conflictful and controversial projects. City Manager Keithley avoided federal programs because he felt that they lacked efficiency and because of his dislike of outside pressure. (Cecil Riley, the present city manager, shares Keithley's views with respect to federal programs.) Both because he has maintained an interest in those programs—particularly those which are related to employment—and because his colleagues in city hall do not share his interest, Mayor Reading has been the city government's spokesman before federal agencies. In trying to influence city and federal officials to take actions in accordance with his goals, a mayor must exercise leadership—that is, he must "make others do something that they would not do otherwise" and that the mayor "specifically wants or intends."[26]

In Oakland, such mayoral leadership is hampered by a forbidding political environment: a city with poverty, unemployment, and racial problems; a city government whose jurisdiction does not include schools, redevelopment, housing, or a wealthy port; a relationship within the government in which the "policy" side is hopelessly outmatched by the "administrative" side; and a city council which habitually deals with problems by giving them away.

This environment would test the mettle of any mayor. But what manner of man is John H. Reading, and how does he use resources available to him? How did his predecessor act differently in the office of mayor? Given the limitations of Oakland's political and governmental system, what could any mayor do? Such an inquiry is important, for a political leader's ability to use internal resources provides some guide to what he will be able to do with outside aid.

THE MAYOR AND HIS USE OF RESOURCES

Political scientists have suggested that personality can have an important impact on political outcomes—particularly if the political actor is located at a critical point in the environment

26 McFarland, *Power and Leadership*, p. 154.

and if that environment is flexible enough to admit of restructuring. Flexibility is increased by conflicting or ambiguous expectations among others about the actor's behavior in his position.[27] By exploring the ways in which Mayor Reading's personality has influenced his methods of leadership, and by comparing his performance to that of his predecessor, we can suggest the extent to which personality makes a difference in the Oakland mayor's office.

John H. Reading's life has been marked by a number of significant successes. From 1940 to 1946, Reading was an Air Force pilot; having served in various command capacities, he attained the rank of lieutenant colonel. Reading then returned to civilian life and entered his family's food processing business, which expanded greatly under his direction. He became president of Ingram Food Products, Inc., Red's Early California Foods, Inc., and several subsidiary companies.

In 1961, Reading was appointed to the city council. Mayor John C. Houlihan, Reading's predecessor, had noticed Reading's attendance at, and participation in, meetings concerned with various neighborhood and civic issues. Feeling that Reading's comments were sensible and that his enthusiasm for "civic involvement" was strong, Houlihan asked Reading if he would like to join the city council. Reading was reluctant at first, but he felt that his advocacy of civic involvement meant that he should take responsibility. (The appointment of a man who · was not active in party politics or political groups, but just an "interested citizen," is indicative of the nonpolitical, non-active-group nature of the Oakland system.) In the spring of 1966, when Mayor Houlihan resigned in the wake of an embezzlement scandal, Reading was chosen by the council as the new mayor. He was overwhelmingly reelected in the elections of 1967, 1969, and 1973.

A Private Man in a Public Office

Discussing the "purist" style in American politics, Nelson Polsby and Aaron Wildavsky state that such a style "represents a virtually complete privatization of politics" in which

---

[27] See Greenstein, "The Impact of Personality," (n. 5 above), pp. 629-641; McFarland, *Power and Leadership*, pp. 183-219.

The private conscience of the leader—rather than his public responsibilities—becomes the focal point of politics. Internal criteria—possession of, devotion to, and standing up for private principles—become the standards of political judgement. Constituents disappear, and we are left with a political leader determining policy on the basis of compatibility with his private principles.[28]

For John H. Reading, standards of conduct which are applicable to men's behavior in private life, embodying values of truthfulness, etiquette, and respect, should also be applicable to the public sphere. If absolute openness is desirable in private life, then it is also desirable in politics. When a black community leader agreed with Mayor Reading on certain issues in private and then attacked the mayor in a public meeting before a black constituency, the mayor felt constrained to remind the community leader—publicly—of all he had said in the "private" meetings. After all, reasoned the mayor, there should be no dividing line between private and public.

Mayor Reading finds himself facing a fundamental dilemma: He is a political leader who does not like politics. Talking about his experience at college and afterward, the mayor remarked:

> I was never interested in political science, or any aspect of the political arena at all. But I am very interested in business and modern management techniques—you know, span of control and that kind of thing. I wanted to put business management into practice in government, and I made a lot of noise about the problems of government. Mayor Houlihan said that if I felt strongly about it I ought to get into politics. And so I got on the City Council.[29]

The Consequences of a Businessman's Approach to Politics

Mayor Reading's attempt to bring private and business standards to bear on politics has had a number of consequences for his behavior as mayor. First of all, this approach has led him to try to simplify politics, to attempt to make governmental action clearer and more rational. Thus, the mayor has consistently argued for the formation of "super-agencies" within the city government which could "coordinate" the tasks of existing

[28] Nelson W. Polsby and Aaron B. Wildavsky, *Presidential Elections* (New York: Charles Scribner's Sons, 1968), p. 180.
[29] Informal remarks at meeting of San Francisco Bay Area Chapter of the American Society for Public Administration, Oakland, October 5, 1967.

departments. (As we have seen, "coordination" is a word whose operational meaning—without the consideration of questions of resources, jurisdiction, and control—remains a mystery. A "public" leader might take the view that "coordination" is not merely a technical problem, that it sometimes involves choosing one set of preferences over others and then enforcing those preferences on other people.)

A second consequence of the mayor's private-business approach to public life is his tendency to define public problems in economic, rather than political, terms:

> I am convinced that employment is a factor of economics much more than of civil rights. Granted, there may be areas of discrimination directly or inadvertently, and we should continue breaking barriers, urging realistic employment standards and emphasizing full opportunity. But in my experience many of the unemployed are just not adequately prepared to take advantage of these opportunities.[30]

In the mayor's view, employment is the key to ending poverty, and the solution to the unemployment problem lies in better education (with vocational counseling to improve the motivation of the poor) and better job training and job development programs.

Another outgrowth of the mayor's private approach to politics is his tendency to deal with political problems in a moralistic way. People who commit nonmoral social actions (and the mayor's definitions are strict) should be punished for them. When City Manager Keithley discussed the possibility in 1969 of levying a tippler's (bar drinker's) tax to help pay the costs of additional Oakland policemen, the mayor responded, "That's only fair. This links the issues nicely! People who drink at bars should bear the costs for protection from crime."

On law and order, the mayor is uncompromising. Crime is a serious threat to our society, and those who are tolerant of criminals—or critical of police—are wittingly or unwittingly aiding and abetting the spread of crime.

But although Mayor Reading often defends the *status quo*, it should not be thought that he is insensitive to individuals' grievances against the government. In fact, his private-business orientation leads him to be suspicious of unrestrained govern-

[30] Remarks before U. S. Civil Rights Commission, May 6, 1967.

ment power. In an effort to aid individuals in their struggles with government bureaucracy, he has fought—unsuccessfully—for an ombudsman plan in Oakland.

Responses to Conflict

Like the city council, Mayor Reading dislikes conflict. "I'm thankful that there's no dissent on our council. When you look at Berkeley, there are enormous divisions." The question that naturally arises is why a man who operates so successfully in the competitive world of business finds it difficult to deal with conflict in politics. Some tentative explanations may be suggested: Mayor Reading's success in his food business was caused in great part by his discovery of a method of manufacturing tamales that was significantly cheaper than his competitors'. Thus, he won a technological competition, not an interpersonal one. Also, when the mayor talks of finding customers for his tamales during his early days in the business, he relates how he drove long distances and worked long hours to contact storeowners and build up his market. Thus, Reading may have been able to outmatch his competition, by thinking quickly and working harder—on his own—rather than by winning interpersonal conflicts.

Recognizing that differences of opinion do exist in public life, Mayor Reading tries to deal with them by using what might be called the "big round table" method. If people could just get together on a personal level, around a table, and talk over their differences, then everything could be settled. In speech after speech, the mayor calls for "total community involvement and cooperation"—among rich and poor, black and white, business and labor. If everyone would cooperate, conflict could be eliminated.

A "public" leader might have much to gain from the recognition of the fact that conflicts exist and may be taken advantage of by leaders. McFarland[31] views leadership in a pluralistic system as an individual's response to multilateral conflict. When conflict increases, set expectations break down and the environment may be manipulated by the leader. A mayor may serve as mediator between conflicting groups; he may seek to

[31] McFarland, *Power and Leadership*, pp. 177ff.

"upgrade the common interest" (as Mayor Lee did in New Haven by creating an urban renewal program that unified otherwise conflicting interests); or he may take advantage of a conflict situation to support the party with whom he agrees. All of these strategies are impossible if the mayor does not recognize, face, and deal with conflict situations.

The problem of current city politics, according to Mayor Reading, is that certain groups—most notably black militants—will not agree to set aside their own selfish interests and work for the community interest. And the losers are inevitably the "large, inactive majority . . . who would like to see real, lasting, and reasonable solutions to our problems."[32]

Confrontation politics has taken a considerable toll on the mayor himself, and he tentatively decided to leave office in 1969 and again in 1973. But both times, he was persuaded to continue by appeals to "civic responsibility."[33]

Now we must ask what Reading can do as mayor, and what a different kind of man might do in this difficult governmental and political structure.

Resources

We have seen that students of urban leadership have focused on the wise use and "pyramiding" of resources as ways in which a political actor can expand his base of power. Because of its structural and staff limitations on the mayor—and perhaps even more because of the lack of organized parties and other political groups available to a political leader—the Oakland political system seems to offer few opportunities for a mayor to pyramid political resources. But a mayor of Oakland does have some resources, or at least potential resources. They are:

[32] Inaugural Address, July 1, 1969.
[33] In an article entitled "Incentives for Political Participation," (*World Politics* 24 [July 1972], pp. 518-546), James L. Payne and Oliver Woshinsky discuss, among other types, politicians who are motivated by an "obligation" incentive. Such people enter politics because they feel a duty to do so, and they are preoccupied with upright conduct in accord with fixed principles. Like Mayor Reading, they do not enjoy politics and have a great distaste for compromise. James David Barber describes a similar type—he calls them "Reluctants"—in his study of Connecticut legislators. The author found that many Reluctants entered politics because of a sense of duty, though they had a distaste for conflict and for politics. See Barber, *The Lawmakers* (New Haven: Yale University Press, 1965), pp. 130-154.

1. *The Mayor's Position as President of the City Council.*—As mayor, Reading presides over public council meetings and private "work sessions." He also appoints council committees. Thus, he has an opportunity to exert a strong influence on the choice of subjects that come up before the council and the ways in which they are discussed and decided.

Former Mayor Houlihan—an outspoken, gregarious lawyer who loved politics—enjoyed this power and exploited it. A careful counter of council votes, he set about to secure outcomes favorable to himself. Houlihan often dispensed favors to friendly councilmen; for example, he gave certain members of the council the opportunity to borrow the mayor's limousine. Once, in order to please a councilman whose chief interest lay in an airport golf course, the mayor created a Golf Course Committee and made the councilman its chairman and only member.

Unlike City Manager Keithley, who used informal council gatherings to strengthen his position with that body, Mayor Reading avoids council dinners and trips with councilmen to ball games at the Coliseum. He appoints council committees on the basis of interest and expertise, and he makes little attempt to influence their deliberations. Further complicating the mayor's task in leading the council is his unwillingness to count votes and to persuade councilmen to see things his way. That would be "pressuring," an activity the mayor does not regard as legitimate.

2. *Power of Appointment.*—The mayor appoints (with the approval of a majority of the council) members of city boards and commissions, including the Housing Authority, Redevelopment Agency, and the Port. He also appoints members of various "mayor's committees," the most active of which is the Citizens' Advisory Committee on Housing.

Throughout the mayor's administration, certain appointees have disappointed him by voting against his favored positions—most notably the Port Commissioners, whose intransigence on employment policies has helped to delay federal EDA projects. "When I first came in," the mayor relates, "I tried to appoint people from opposite points of view." But after three years, he had become "much more cynical." His new policy: "I appoint people who represent my point of view."

When the mayor has decided on those people who represent his point of view, he still has to get them approved by the city council. And council approval is by no means automatic. In July 1968, the city council refused to approve the mayor's reappointment of two members of the Planning Commission—one of them the chairman. At the same time, the mayor's move to replace an anti-Reading councilman's business associate as head of the Housing Authority failed when the man refused to leave his post and was backed up by the council. In neither of these cases was Mayor Reading willing to fight on the council or in the newspapers for his appointments.

3. *Prestige.*—Describing the success of Mayor Lee of New Haven, Dahl shows how the mayor was able to use his personal popularity and prestige to extract concessions from other political and business leaders.[34] Richard Neustadt suggests that "popular prestige" in the form of "public standing" is a source of influence for a president in his dealings with people in Washington. This is because political actors depend on the public for votes and support.[35]

Mayor Reading has had an enviable electoral record, amassing over 80 percent of the vote in his reelection campaign of 1967 and gaining over 60 percent in 1969 and 1973. The prestige that results from electoral success in the city's highest elective office might be turned into an important resource; Mayor Lee was certainly able to capitalize on his success at the polls. But in Oakland, the lack of interest in electoral politics renders this resource less valuable. For leaders to be influenced by the resource of popular prestige, they must be convinced that public opinion can somehow have an impact on them. The mayor has used the prestige of his office to good advantage in certain instances: in organizing business leaders into a campaign for a school tax, in promoting support for a downtown hotel and convention center, and in leading the campaign for a new charter. But on the whole, the mayor has tended to underutilize this potential resource. For the existence of prestige without the willingness to use the next named resource, publicity, may not be sufficient to accomplish mayoral goals.

4. *Publicity.*—In a discussion of "Protest as a Political Re-

[34] Dahl, *Who Governs?* p. 308-310.
[35] Richard Neustadt, *Presidential Power* (New York: John Wiley, 1960), pp. 86ff.

source," Michael Lipsky demonstrates how important publicity is to "low resource" political actors who lack money, staff, and stable organizational foundations:

> The communications media are extremely powerful in city politics. In granting or withholding publicity, in determining what information most people will have on most issues, and what alternatives they will consider in response to issues, the media truly, as Norton Long has put it, "set . . . the civic agenda." Like the tree falling unheard in the forest, there is no protest unless protest is perceived and projected.[36]

In a similar manner, there is no mayoral leadership in Oakland unless that leadership is perceived and projected. Although the mayor is obviously in a better position than most protest groups to influence policy, his limited jurisdictional and staff resources make him dependent, to a great extent, on media publicity to make his views known and to influence people to follow them. The mayor has certain advantages in using publicity. Unlike most protest groups, he has a consistently high legitimacy and an automatic visibility. Furthermore, in Oakland, John Reading has a friendly newspaper in the *Tribune* This aspect of the political environment, at least, appears favorable to mayoral leadership and resource-building.

However, the mayor's essentially private nature and his preference for quiet and rational discussion make him less than eager to take his case on public matters to the people through the news media. In a number of his disputes with both city and federal actors, he has accepted defeat rather than attempting to use publicity in a strategic way.

Publicity is a resource which is not severely limited by considerations of formal structure and jurisdiction, and an enterprising mayor can make good use of the media. Mayor Houlihan had a ten-minute weekly radio program through which he told Bay Area listeners about his activities and the governmental issues in Oakland. When the city council refused to endorse a bond issue for Bay Area Rapid Transit, Houlihan came out publicly for the issue anyway. The bond campaign was successful in a close election; a switch of 2,000 votes in Oakland would have defeated the issue. In this resource area, a "public" personality can make a difference.

[36] Michael Lipsky, "Protest as a Political Resource," *The American Political Science Review* 62 (December 1968), p. 1151.

Underutilization and Dispersion of Resources

Operating in a low-resource environment, Mayor Reading has tended to underutilize the political resources he has. For example, the mayor's failure to count votes and to use persuasion has caused him to gain less than full advantage from his role as president of the council. Instead of pyramiding resources, it often appears that the mayor is engaged in a practice of *resource dispersion*, failing to combine his resources with each other. Thus, his power of appointment has been blocked by his failure to lead the council and to use publicity; and the mayor's personal prestige has been underutilized because of his unwillingness to take issues to the public. Except for occasional pronouncements on law and order, the mayor's private style has led him to avoid the public spotlight. For a low-resource political actor with high legitimacy, such avoidance seems extremely unwise.

Personal Opportunities in Spite of Structure

Although governmental and political structures set limits on what any mayor can do, personality can make a difference. On the basis of Mayor Houlihan's experience and studies of successful leadership elsewhere, we can suggest some of the ways in which a more politically oriented mayor might use his leadership resources in Oakland. In *The Washington Community 1800-1828*,[37] James S. Young describes a situation in the nation's capital at that time which appears remarkably similar to that in Oakland today: a lack of active groups; apathy and indifference among the populace; fragmented social subgroups formed around separate branches of government, with few integrating forces; weak congressional parties; an antipolitical ideology, even among politicians; and an absence of presidential staff. Here, according to Young, the personality of the president made a difference. For "the President had to improvise out of wit and ingenuity, as his political talents, circumstances, statutes, and good fortune permitted."[38] During the period studied, only Jefferson was successful enough at "statecraft" to be able to provide leadership. One of Jefferson's

[37] (New York: Columbia University Press, 1966).
[38] *Ibid.*, p. 159.

prime tools of statecraft was "social lobbying"—the wining and dining of legislators at the White House. Personal charm and persuasion could triumph, even in a situation where the president had few resources. Jefferson also utilized publicity, through the medium of a presidential "newspaper"—a journal published by a friend of the president, which faithfully carried the president's views.

A mayor of Oakland can also use "social lobbying" and personal persuasion as techniques to influence councilmen to follow his leadership. Mayor Houlihan attended council social occasions and provided favors, like the use of the mayoral limousine, that councilmen could appreciate. And when he could not control the city council on a particular issue, Houlihan used publicity to take his case to the citizens of Oakland. The mayor's radio program was the counterpart to a presidential newspaper.

Faced by the limitations of the city's low resource position, an aggressive mayor of Oakland can attempt to use his persuasive power on outside governmental bodies in an attempt to expand city resources. Thus, Mayor Houlihan persuaded the Alameda County supervisors to grant $35,000 from county highway funds to build a tunnel under the new Oakland Museum. Houlihan appeared to delight in testing his art of persuasion on anyone who could bring more resources to Oakland or to him.

Although mayors of Oakland are limited both by governmental structure and political disorganization, there are still opportunities for an inventive political person to make the most of the situation by social lobbying, persuasion, and publicity. Furthermore, to supplement strained city resources a mayor can seek funds from outside. Thus, federal funds might be able to provide initial resources for a mayor to use in creating others.

These kinds of activities represent ways in which a leader without many resources can operate. However, the tasks of social lobbying, persuasion, and publicizing can be very difficult and distasteful for a basically private person like John Reading. His personality has made a difference in his ability to exert leadership in the mayor's office.

Because Mayor Reading is not only the chief elected official in Oakland's city government, but also the official in that government who has involved himself most extensively in bargaining with federal agencies, his personality and his method of using resources have had implications for the course of federal programs in the city. We shall return to that topic in later chapters.

CONCLUSION: LEADERSHIP AND THE POLITICAL SYSTEM

Conditions of Leadership in Oakland: An Assessment

Although calls for mayoral leadership fill the literature on city politics,[39] an understanding of such leadership in any given city requires an examination of the political environment, the personalities involved, and the ways in which the mayor uses the resources available to him.

It is clear that the leadership exercised by Mayor John Reading of Oakland does not closely approximate the model of leadership described earlier—the model of a political leader who sets goals and then uses a wide variety of means to influence others to act according to his own preferences. This is due both to environmental and personal factors.

The model listed seven environmental requirements which a mayor would need to exercise effective leadership, and it is obvious that the Oakland governmental and political structure provides little comfort for any mayor. Like most cities, Oakland faces a revenue strain and rising personnel costs—which means that it does not have (a) *sufficient financial resources* with which a mayor can launch innovative social programs. Nor does the city have (b) *jurisdiction* in the vital program areas of education, housing, and redevelopment. Under the council-manager form of government, there are severe limits to (c) *mayoral jurisdiction within the city government.* And the mayor has neither (d) sufficient *salary* nor (e) adequate *staff* (one administrative assistant and three secretaries) to perform as a full-time and well-informed official.

[39] See, for example, Alexander L. George, "Political Leadership" (n. 2 above), p. 1197, and the *Report of the National Advisory Commission on Civil Disorders* (New York: Bantam, 1968), p. 298.

Although Oakland does provide the mayor with (f) *a ready vehicle of publicity* in the *Oakland Tribune*, the rest of the political environment offers him little comfort. There are few (g) *politically oriented groups* that can provide support for a mayoral program.

Without governmental jurisdiction, staff, and financial resources, it is hard for any mayor to direct, or even influence, the actions of others. But it is not true that mayoral leadership is impossible in Oakland. For the mayor does have certain resources (position as presiding officer, power of appointment, prestige, legitimacy), and an adept political actor can pyramid those resources. John Houlihan, a man who enjoyed the turbulence of the public arena, was able to build on his meager mayoral resources. But John Reading, a private man with a distaste for conflict and a preference for quiet discussion, has consistently underutilized his political resources. In Oakland, a mayor's lot is not a happy one, but it is not a hopeless one, either.

The Political System and Its Influence on Leadership

In Oakland, as in other cities, the mayor is the product of the political system. The nature of that system has a significant influence on the kinds of people who become mayor and the forms of leadership they can exercise. In the nongroup, nonpartisan, noninterested, and non-electoral political system of Oakland, it is entirely possible for a "nonpolitical" civic reformer like John Reading to attain the position of mayor without really trying for it. No groups, parties, or politicians could make an effective claim on the office.

Not only does the political and governmental system have an influence on what kind of person becomes mayor and how much time he can spend on his job; that system has an impact on the forms of mayoral leadership that are possible.

The lack of administrative authority, financial resources, and staff which is a part of the governmental system means that the leadership most often possible is hortatory in nature (encouraging voters to pass a bond issue or charter reform, for example). In the absence of administrative authority, the exercise of hortatory leadership can ultimately be frustrating to the mayor. (Thus, Mayor Reading successfully urged the voters to approve charter reform, but he had little voice in the critical implementation of that reform.)

Even more important in determining the nature of mayoral leadership is the nature of the political system in the city itself. The neighboring city of Berkeley, which has a formal governmental system similar to Oakland's, has witnessed the formation, passage, and implementation of an extensive program of municipal legislation covering the fields of public works, health care, and equal employment opportunity, among others. This program was framed by a political caucus which gathered together a number of strong liberal and civic groups and supported municipal candidates pledged to a particular program. (It took a number of hotly contested elections to achieve victory.)

In Oakland, by contrast, the lack of strong groups and parties means that the mayor does not have sustained and consistent backing in the public for policies he advocates. Furthermore, because business and labor leaders have shown so little interest in city affairs, the mayor has little opportunity to discover their thinking on various issues. As a result, leadership becomes not only hortatory, but sharply divorced from the policy preferences of relevant urban leaders. Thus, in the spring of 1970, when Mayor Reading suggested that National Guard troops might be called to operate buses in the midst of a strike, the proposal was sharply criticized by both labor and management.

If electoral competition is non-existent, there is no incentive for groups of councilmen to join together in framing a program. If no boats are rocked, then no competition may surface. Contested elections, which can have the effect of defining alternatives and building support for those alternatives, might provide both a start and a direction for the victors. The exercise of leadership in a virtually non-electoral system runs the risk of being rudderless.

Of course, the lack of leadership in the mayor's office does not mean that no leadership is being exerted in the urban political system The city manager certainly exerts leadership within the city administration, and, as we shall see, the federal government encouraged the development of alternative power

centers in the poor, black community. It is certainly true that
the weak position of elected political leaders in Oakland has
aided the growth of leadership in other arenas. In the next
chapter, I will discuss the federally supported arena and its
relationship to the electoral arena.

It is important to point out here that there are significant
potential differences between leadership exerted by elected
politicians and leadership exerted by others. For citizens have
regular opportunities to change their elected leaders, and with
these opportunities come certain possible means of influencing
the actions of those leaders. Neither the city manager, nor a
port commissioner, nor the poverty program director is subject
to the possibility of this kind of direct and widespread popular
control. A city administrator may be responsive to people's
wishes if he decides that this is a wise policy. But, if elections
are competitive, a mayor or councilman has a greater incentive
to be responsive, because his continued maintenance in office
depends on it.

Another difference between elected and non-elected leaders
is that people *expect* elected leaders to be more responsive than
non-elected leaders. Almond and Verba found that Americans
(in contrast to Germans or Italians) are far more likely to
contact elected political officials than they are to contact non-
elected administrative officials if they want to influence their
local government.[40] Perhaps visibility has a lot to do with
citizens' propensity to contact elected officials. Oakland Project
interviews conducted in 1969 showed that few Oakland citizens
knew *what* a city manager was, let alone the identity of the
present incumbent.

Though governmental structure, dependence on independent
groups, and personality traits can all exert constraints on
leadership, competitive elections might provide a constraint
more directly linked to popular preferences. Besides providing
a link from the populace to a leader, electoral activity can
provide a vehicle for mobilizing the resource of numbers
against other resources like money or social standing or control
of communications media. The lack of power on the part of

---

[40] Gabriel A. Almond and Sidney Verba, *The Civic Culture* (Boston: Little, Brown,
1965), p. 148.

elected officials may lead to more power for those who presently hold these other resources.

Of course, the electoral link is far from automatic. The extent to which numbers of people *can* influence elected leaders is dependent upon the electoral and political system of a particular city. At-large elections in Oakland make the task of minority candidates more difficult. And without interested and active political groups in the city, it has been hard to mount any credible campaign for a nonincumbent. Appointment politics has meant that there is usually a full supply of incumbents. If elections are noncompetitive, the incumbents have no real incentive to build constituencies or to be responsive to citizens' wishes. Under these conditions, the potential of elections for influencing the actions of leaders is unrealized.

Thus, the lack of political groups, organized parties, and contested elections has a clear effect on the behavior of those people who are elected. In such a system, it is difficult for those officials who are interested in exercising leadership to find out about citizens' policy preferences and to build support for their own. Without contested elections, there is little incentive for politicians to join together in creating programs.

The nature of the local political system, besides influencing the selection and behavior of officials within the city, also has important implications for the relationship between the city and the federal government. Because federal-city relations involve mutual dependence, with the federal government relying on local groups to implement its programs, those programs will be influenced by the kinds of political relationships that exist in a city.

Of course, the relationship works both ways; federal activity has an impact on a city's public life. By bringing in both financial resources and rules that regulate the use of those resources, federal agencies cannot avoid having an effect in local political processes. Indeed, some federal agencies have consciously attempted to produce changes in the structure of urban politics. The next chapter will focus on federal programs which stimulated a challenge to the city government itself.

3

Federal Political Impact:
The Creation of a New Arena

Having examined the political landscape of Oakland, let us move to a consideration of the federal impact on the city's political system. This chapter will focus on the creation—by federal poverty and employment program funding—of a new arena for political action, which has existed outside the city's electoral arena. (I have earlier defined arena as "a site at which the exchange of political resources takes place." At such sites, political actors may bargain with each other for a variety of scarce resources: jobs, money, authority over programs, control over instruments of physical force, and so forth.) Although federal money has gone to a wide range of institutions in Oakland, the creation and maintenance of this new site of political activity—and the relations between its occupants and city officials—occupied the center stage of public debate and controversy in the city from 1967 to 1971.

After charting the patterns of federal funding in Oakland,

I will identify and examine three factors that facilitated the creation of a separate arena: federal policy, avoidance behavior on the part of the city council and city manager, and the mayor's underutilization of his political resources. Because political arenas are not empty spaces, and because the structure of incentives and rewards that exists in an arena tends to have an influence on the kinds of behavior that will occur within it, I will compare the incentive structures of the federal program and city electoral arenas. I will argue that the two arenas differ in the kinds of behavior they encourage and in the long-term benefits they offer to political actors within them. Finally, with reference to the Oakland experience, I will suggest that there are considerable obstacles to movement from the federal program arena to the more permanent electoral arena.

THE PATTERN OF FEDERAL FUNDING: A SMALL SHARE FOR CITY GOVERNMENT

As I stated at the outset, the amount of federal funds flowing into Oakland has been substantial. Figures for 1968 (a year in which the city budget totalled $57.9 million) showed that the total nondefense federal spending in the city was $95.5 million; if defense expenditures were added, the figure jumped to $487.4 million. (See Table 2 in Chapter 1.)

An examination of the allocation of these funds among local recipients demonstrates how small City Hall's share was. Table 9 shows the leading local institutional recipients of federal grants in 1968.

The distribution of federal funding reflects the fragmentation and dispersion of governmental authority discussed in the last chapter. City government's share, representing about 1 percent of total nondefense spending in the city, was made up of an urban planning grant to the City Planning Department ($368,-531), "open spaces" grants to the Recreation Department ($358,292), money for the Oakland Public Library to extend its services to Mexican-Americans ($100,000), and water and sewer facilities grants to the Street and Engineering Department ($182,500).[1]

[1] All figures for federal funding are taken from the *Digest of Current Federal Programs in the City of Oakland, 1968.*

Table 9: Leading Institutional Recipients of Nondefense Grants in
Oakland, 1968: The Modest Share of City Government

Local recipient institution	Dollar amount received
Alameda County Welfare Department (for Oakland cases)...	$19,472,154
Oakland Redevelopment Agency	6,635,115
Oakland Economic Development Council, Inc..............	5,210,398
Peralta Junior College District..........................	4,692,182
Bay Area Rapid Transit District (for Oakland segment)......	4,240,000
Oakland Unified School District.........................	2,579,063
Oakland Housing Authority	1,522,995
City of Oakland	1,009,323
Highland General Hospital...............................	699,979
Alameda County Health Department (special poverty project for Oakland)................	425,771

Source: *Digest of Current Federal Programs in the City of Oakland,* prepared for
Mayor John H. Reading by Jeffrey L. Pressman, October, 1968.

Grants to autonomous governmental bodies such as the
Redevelopment Agency (which received funds for a number
of ongoing and planned redevelopment projects) and the Housing Authority (with funds for the provision and management
of low-cost housing units) easily exceeded the share received
by city government. But much more disturbing to Mayor
Reading was the $5.2 million share received by the Oakland
Economic Development Council, Inc., the Community Action
Agency of the poverty program. From 1967, when OEDCI
declared its independence from City Hall, to 1971, when the
federal government cut off its funding, the poverty agency was
a federally financed organization both independent of City Hall
and hostile to it.

OEDCI received funds for two major programs. $1.7 million
was made up of OEO funding for a range of community action
programs. Approximately half of this money was delegated by
OEDCI to other agencies for the administration of social
programs for the poor. For example, the Alameda County
Health Department was given funds for the operation of family
planning clinics and denal programs. The Legal Aid Society
of Alameda County received money for the provision of legal
services to poor people; and the Children's Vision Center of
the East Bay was delegated the responsibility for operating
a program of vision care for poverty residents. The remainder

of the community action funding was administered by OEDCI itself—for program planning, neighborhood organization, and neighborhood service centers. Thus, OEDCI was not only spending money for social services; it was also carrying on a program of political organization in the poverty community.

The bulk of federal funding for OEDCI came not from OEO, but from the Department of Labor. For OEDCI had been chosen as the prime sponsor of the Concentrated Employment Program, which provided money for job training, remedial education, job placement, and the supervision of work experience. In 1968, OEDCI received $3.5 million under that program. This was a particularly bitter blow to Mayor Reading, who had made employment programs his major policy concern and who badly wanted the Concentrated Employment Program to be lodged in City Hall.

Thus, substantial federal funding was going to a local organization which was openly hostile to city government. And that body was carrying on an active program of neighborhood organization in the ghettoes of the city. For black leaders, there was a new arena in which they could engage in political action.

The Sources of a Separate Arena

How was the federal government able to bypass City Hall in providing funding to this new and independent arena? In part, the answer to this question lies in the "maximum feasible participation of the poor" approach of the federal government[2] and in OEDCI's own tenacity in fighting for funding. But the policy outcomes were also strongly influenced by the characteristic behavior patterns of Oakland's city officials, which were explored in chapter 2. Avoidance behavior on the part of city councilmen and administrators, as well as underutilization of political resources on the part of the mayor, played a large part in city government's failure to achieve control over federal funding in this area. (Again, because the mayor has been the

[2] For a treatment of the development of this approach, see Richard Blumenthal, "The Bureaucracy: Antipoverty and the Community Action Program," in *American Political Institutions and Public Policy*, ed. Allan P. Sindler (Boston: Little, Brown, 1969), pp. 128-179.

city official most interested in federal social programs and in gaining jurisdiction over them, I will pay particular attention to his actions.) Let us move now to a consideration of the various factors leading to the creation of a separate political arena.

Federal Decisions Provide Local Opportunities

Policy decisions by federal actors provided the structural framework and political resources which local actors were able to use in building a new political arena. The Economic Opportunity Act of 1964 stated that community action programs should be "developed, conducted, and administered with the maximum feasible participation of residents of the areas and members of the groups served."[3] When the federal war on poverty came to Oakland in 1964, the citizens' advisory committee of the Ford Foundation Grey Areas Program—a body which included a number of minority group representatives—was transformed into the Oakland Economic Development Council, the principal decision-making body for the poverty program.[4]

At its beginning, Oakland's poverty program was joined to the city government. The twenty-five members of OEDC were appointed by the mayor, and the poverty council's staff was located in the city government's newly created Department of Human Resources. Because of pressures from poverty target areas for direct representation, OEDC provided in 1965 for eight additional council members to be selected by poverty neighborhood groups. OEDC was also responding to regional OEO guidelines of March 1965, which required representation from target areas on the policy making body of the community action program.[5] But during the beginning stages of OEDC activities, black professionals—who sat among the "at large" members appointed by the mayor—continued to play a dominant role

[3] *Economic Opportunity Act of 1964*, 88th Congress, 2nd Session, Section 202 (a).
[4] In examining the development of Oakland's poverty program, I have found the work of my Oakland Project colleague, Judith V. May, most useful. See her "Two Model Cities: Political Development on the Local Level" (Paper delivered at the Annual Meeting of the American Political Science Association, 1969).
[5] See the case study of OEDC in Ralph M. Kramer, *Participation of the Poor* (Englewood Cliffs, N. J.: Prentice-Hall, 1969), pp. 108-149.

in the decisions of that body. Judith May has pointed out that these professionals utilized the strategy of "responsible opposition" to the city which they had developed as civil rights leaders. Through control over poverty funds, they hoped to increase their effectiveness in negotiating with established agencies over the quality of services delivered to poor people. These poverty program leaders attempted to carry on negotiations in an atmosphere of "responsibility" and with an absence of open conflict between the city and the poor.[6]

The dominance of the black professionals was eventually challenged by the target area representatives, who began to unite around the issue of securing greater representation and authority within OEDC and its executive committee.[7] At an OEDC program review meeting on March 12, 1966, target area members walked out after demanding that the OEDC give them "51 percent control" over the board and allocate more of its money to the poor than to agency professionals.[8] The matter was referred to a special study committee, and the OEDC eventually adopted that committee's recommendation that target area representatives should constitute 51 percent of the governing council.

Spurred by its poverty area members, the OEDC began to adopt a more hostile stance toward City Hall. In December 1965, the poverty council proposed the creation of a police review board, and this issue precipitated a bitter dispute with the city council. Conflicts during 1966 over the sponsorship of the federal Concentrated Employment Program and Neighborhood Centers Pilot Program (both to be discussed later) further widened the gap between the OEDC and the city government. Finally, in August 1967, the OEDC voted to sever its attachment to the city and become an independent nonprofit corporation, the Oakland Economic Development Council, Incorporated. Executive director Dr. Norvel Smith, an advocate of negotiation with city agencies, resigned. He was replaced by Percy Moore, a man who rejected the negotiating strategy and urged the poverty agency to use its funds to create an independent political base. Operating from such a base, Moore

[6] See May, "Two Model Cities," p. 14.
[7] Kramer, *Participation of the Poor*, pp. 117ff.
[8] May, "Two Model Cities," p. 14.

argued, poverty leaders could extract concessions that agencies were unwilling to make.[9] Under Moore's direction, the poverty board started moving away from a "service" orientation and toward a "political organization" thrust. The poverty program in Oakland had become both separate from and hostile to City Hall.

Not only had federal decisions, by requiring "participation of the poor," created the framework for organizing the new arena; further federal actions provided the resources of money and jobs which allowed the arena to grow. In the case of both the Neighborhood Centers Pilot Program (NCPP) and the Concentrated Employment Program (CEP), federal officials bypassed City Hall to lodge local sponsorship with the OEDC. I will show in chapter 5 how the NCPP decision provoked arguments among federal agencies; here I will concentrate on CEP.

This comprehensive manpower program, which was administered by the Department of Labor, contained funds for job training, job placement, and remedial education. When the program was being discussed in Oakland in early 1967, Mayor Reading felt that his newly created manpower commission would be the natural local sponsor of a federal manpower effort. After all, the commission was being encouraged and financially aided by the federal Economic Development Administration. But federal policy favored Community Action Agencies as prime sponsors of CEP (a concession given by Labor to OEO in return for Labor's gaining administrative responsibility for the program), and the OEDC was given control of the new manpower program in Oakland. It is not clear whether federal officials ever told the mayor about the general federal policy favoring Community Action Agencies, and no apparent thought on the federal level was given to the strained relations between the city government and the poverty program.[10] Reading had believed that the question of designation was open, and he was shocked by the final decision. Lacking authority over this central employment effort, members of the manpower commis-

[9] *Ibid.*, p. 16.

[10] Oakland Task Force, Federal Executive Board, *An Analysis of Federal Decision-Making and Impact: The Federal Government in Oakland* (San Francisco, 1968; New York: Praeger, 1970), pp. 119-120; 127.

sion eventually lost interest in their own organization and it began to wither away, leaving only a skeleton staff.

After making this initial manpower program commitment to the poverty council, federal officials steadfastly refused to alter their policy in response to subsequent pleas from City Hall. When fellow-Republican Richard Nixon was elected President in 1968, Mayor Reading (who had headed California Mayors for Nixon) hoped for a change in federal attitude toward Oakland city government. But numerous mayoral letters and personal visits were to no avail, as CEP funds continued to flow to the separate poverty arena. When the mayor requested federal officials to (a) change the guidelines that made Community Action Agencies the presumptive prime sponsors of CEP and (b) provide the city with the administrative staff necessary to supervise a manpower program, a federal manpower administrator replied that (a) current federal guidelines favored OEDCI as prime sponsor and that (b) the city did not have the administrative capacity to run the program.[11]

What the federal government gives, it can also take away—as OEDCI learned to its sorrow. In April 1971, following a declaration by Percy Moore that he would use agency funds to run campaigns against city council incumbents, national OEO upheld Governor Reagan's veto of OEDCI funding.[12] (The governor's office, relying on a report by state OEO, had charged that Moore's staff had intimidated poverty council members, misused funds, and failed to act on complaints of political activity on the part of its members.) Thus, a federal decision eventually dealt a crushing blow to OEDCI.

Still, by a series of decisions starting with the passage of the Economic Opportunity Act in 1964, the federal government had provided both an organizing focus and subsequent financial resources for poverty program activists in Oakland. The role of federal actors in creating and sustaining the new arena was thus considerable.

City Officials' Avoidance Behavior

Another factor contributing to the creation of a separate

[11] Letter from Arnold R. Weber, Assistant Secretary of Labor for Manpower, to Mayor Reading, May 28, 1969.
[12] *Oakland Tribune*, April 13, 1971.

political arena came from within Oakland's political system—
the characteristic tendency of city councilmen and administrators to avoid conflict and controversy. As we have seen in the
last chapter, these men strive to define their jurisdiction narrowly and even to give away authority in issue areas that are
perceived as troublesome.

In the turbulent environment of federal social programs, this
tendency toward avoidance has been marked. When the Green
Amendment was passed by Congress in 1967,[13] it appeared to
give city officials an opportunity for increased leverage over
the poverty program. Under the amendment, local governments
were given the power to "designate" a Community Action
Agency for their community, or to run the program themselves.
Furthermore, one third of the poverty board would consist of
local officials. Even though Mayor Reading did not seriously
consider taking over the poverty program at that time, he hoped
that these new provisions would give him sufficient bargaining
power to demand a role in the manpower program, in which
he had a particular interest.

But once again, the "shrinking violet" behavior of Oakland
city officials appeared and blocked any move to expand city
jurisdiction. Neither the city council nor the manager wanted
anything to do with taking over the turbulent poverty agency,
and they responded coolly to Reading's discussion of the Green
Amendment as an "opportunity." Then City Attorney Goggin
advised the mayor that the Green Amendment could not really
be used to take over the poverty program, anyway. He argued
that, even if the city government chose to operate the program
itself, it would have to appoint a board which would then
become independent. Besides, the charter says that the city
council shall have no administrative powers; therefore, reasoned the attorney, it would be impossible for the elected
officials of Oakland to operate a poverty program under the
amendment. Discouraged by the indifference of his colleagues,
Mayor Reading wrote to Congresswoman Green to tell her of
the difficulties he had encountered in implementing her amendment.

[13] U.S. Congress, *Economic Opportunity Amendments of 1967,* 90th Congress, 1st
Session, Sections 210ff.

Even when national OEO finally cut off funding for the OEDCI, thus simplifying the process of City Hall takeover, the city council showed no immediate inclination to take on added responsibility. The council responded to the federal government's veto by creating a "City Council-citizens task force" which in turn recommended that the state take over the program "temporarily."[14] But the state blocked the city council's attempt to give away authority by suddenly announcing that it would be unable to take over Oakland's antipoverty operations, even on an interim basis.[15] Meanwhile, the Oakland program remained in limbo while the city council tried to decide whether to operate the program itself, create a new nonprofit corporation, or redesignate the OEDCI (minus Percy Moore). If this was a victory for City Hall, it was not one that was greatly appreciated by the inhabitants of that building. Much to Mayor Reading's distress, city officials continued to shrink from involvement in this turbulent social program. Finally, with the other alternatives seemingly blocked, the city council initiated steps to take over the poverty program—at least until an acceptable independent agency could be found.[16] The council was expanding its authority, but with extreme reluctance.

City officials' avoidance behavior was also evident in the manpower program area. The city manager's office was not enthusiastic about even a small manpower commission and staff, let alone about providing the office space, personnel, and administrative guidance required for a major effort. And the city council shared this lack of enthusiasm. Its Ways and Means Committee recommended in 1968 that the manpower commission be cut from the budget. Federal administrators argued that the city government could not receive manpower programs until it demonstrated the capacity to support them, but the mayor could not convince other city officials to create that support. Faced with the turbulence of federal social programs, city councilmen and administrators tended to limit their jurisdiction in order to avoid conflict. This pattern of behavior helped make it possible for other local actors to take control

---

[14] *Oakland Tribune*, April 20, 1971.
[15] *Ibid.*, April 29, 1971.
[16] *Ibid.*, May 5, 1971.

of federal programs and to operate them separately from City Hall.

Underutilization of Mayoral Resources

Unlike his counterparts in city government, Mayor Reading has not shrunk from involvement in federal programs. But his inability to use his political resources effectively proved to be another factor facilitating the maintenance of a separate political arena in Oakland. In chapter 2, I outlined a number of traits which caused the mayor to make less than full use of his resources: inability to separate public from private life; unwillingness to plan and carry out legislative strategies; inability to recognize, utilize, and deal with conflict; and reluctance to persuade and use publicity. I will now show how these same personality traits helped to frustrate the mayor's attempts to bring federal programs under City Hall control.

Mayor Reading's characteristic insistence on the morality of announcing one's private preferences in public discussion has worked to his disadvantage in his relations with the poverty program. After his colleagues in City Hall had demonstrated their lack of enthusiasm for taking over the program in 1968, Reading made one last attempt to capitalize on the designation power of the Green Amendment. In May of that year, he asked the city council to withhold designation "until OEDC had solved its leadership problems"—that is, until the OEDC fired its militantly anti-City Hall director, Percy Moore. At this time, poverty council members themselves were becoming increasingly resentful of Moore's centralization of authority in the hands of agency staff, and Moore's continued existence in his job was threatened. But the mayor's move served to shore up Moore's somewhat shaky position on the OEDCI council by making his retention a question of poverty program independence, pride, and racial solidarity. Reading's openness in announcing his private feelings had caused him to lose ground in pursuing a public goal.

The mayor's unwillingness to plan legislative strategies and count votes also weakened him in his dealings with actors in the poverty arena. In the summer of 1968, Percy Moore's opponents on the OEDCI board came within two votes (14-12) of unseating the executive director. A city councilman who was one of the mayor's "public official" appointments to the poverty board told the mayor that he had voted for Moore because he "didn't feel it was an important vote." If he had known it was important, the councilman told Reading, he "might have changed." And if the mayor had counted votes and attempted to instruct his delegates, it is quite possible that the result might have been different. (It must be pointed out that the mayor did learn from this experience; in 1969 he was careful to appoint as his representatives to OEDCI only people who would pledge to vote to fire Moore.)

Another personality trait that weakened mayoral influence on federal programs was Reading's inability to recognize conflict and utilize it in his own interest. During the early years of the poverty program, Reading held to the belief that good will and rational discussion could eliminate conflicts between the OEDC and the city; he was shocked by the open break that developed. Given the existence of sharply opposing interests, the mayor's "big round table" method of conflict resolution (discussed in chapter 2) proved inadequate. When certain federal officials in the Department of Labor backed Reading's attempts to gain more control over poverty and employment programs, the mayor held back from joining these officials in challenging OEO and OEDCI. With his distaste for federal fragmentation and competition, Reading preferred to wait for a unified federal decision in his favor.

Finally, the mayor's unwillingness to use persuasion and publicity to gain his ends put him at a disadvantage in the competition for federal programs. In contrast to Percy Moore, who called frequent press conferences to explain his agency's need for money, Mayor Reading endured his defeats in relative silence. Federal officials might have been less willing to ignore a mayor who would publicize what he saw as national slights to local government. Mayoral underutilization of political resources helped make it possible for federal actors to overlook City Hall and provide funds to a separate arena outside it.

Thus, although federal policy decisions—and the advantage that local poverty actors took of them—constituted an important source of the new political arena, other sources of that arena are to be found in the characteristic behavior of Oakland's

city officials. It would be a mistake to attribute these political
outcomes merely to the personal idiosyncracies of Mayor Reading and other local officials. For, as we have seen in the last
chapter, the political system exerts a strong influence on the
kinds of people who hold public office and the kinds of behavior
they exhibit there. Oakland's nongroup political system and
the part-time nature of political positions constitute constraints to leadership.

Federal Programs and Local Political Leadership

In both the poverty program and employment policy areas,
the same environmental and personal elements which limited
mayoral leadership within the city system prevented Mayor
Reading from using federal funding to advance his program
initiatives. Outside aid cannot by itself generate viable political
leadership in local government; if the organizational and personal bases for such leadership are lacking, then outside assistance may not even be able to be attracted and used..H. Douglas
Price, in his review of *Who Governs?*, has suggested that it
was not so much the skill of local political leaders (as Dahl
had suggested it was) that accounted for New Haven's success
in redevelopment, but rather the massive infusion of federal
aid.[17] But a community's reliance on federal funding does not
really lessen the importance of local political leaders in the
process. For, as the New Haven and Oakland experiences show,
there is tremendous variability in the capacity of local officials
to attract and exploit federal funding.[18]

Although some federal decisions were clearly designed to
bypass City Hall in setting up programs, there were certain
federal agencies and officials who tried to work through the
mayor to achieve their objectives. For example, HUD officials
tried to enlist the mayor's help in encouraging Oakland's
Housing Authority and Redevelopment Agency to move more
quickly in executing projects. Economic Development Admin-

---

[17] H. Douglas Price, Review of *Who Governs?* by Robert A. Dahl, *Yale Law Journal*
71 (1962), p. 1593.
[18] The variability of political actors' capacity to exploit federal resources is noted
in Russell D. Murphy, *Political Entrepreneurs and Urban Poverty: The Formative
Years of New Haven's Model Anti-Poverty Project* (Lexington, Mass.: Heath-Lexington
Books, 1971).

istration representatives counted on Mayor Reading to exert pressure on local businessmen to hire the hard-core unemployed and to fulfill other obligations on EDA projects. And field representatives of the Labor Department urged the mayor to be more aggressive in his use of the city's manpower effort. In all these cases, federal expectations of strong local support were not realized; the mayor's style of political behavior was not changed by the mere fact of federal support. And the structural obstacles to the exertion of leadership in Oakland—as well as the mayor's inability to use his resources skillfully—became liabilities for the federal agencies as well. The connection between federal program outcomes and local political support is a close one.

THE TWO ARENAS CONTRASTED

Based on her study of early negotiations over the model cities program in Oakland, in which West Oakland ghetto residents won both majority representation on the program's steering committee and the right of veto (along with the city council) of steering committee decisions, Judith May saw "the creation of a second government for the West Oakland community. West Oakland residents, in effect, declared their independence from the authority of the local government and established new institutions which they vested with legitimacy."[19]

In fact, through their attraction of and control over federal funding in the poverty program and employment areas, black community based organizations had already created an arena in which individual actors and groups were battling for authority, money, and status. Still, although federal programs have stimulated participation in the poor black community and have provided resources with which black leaders can attempt to organize in ghetto neighborhoods, the arena that such programs have created cannot be regarded as a substitute for the city's electoral politics arena. For these two forums for decision-making differ in some important ways.

[19] May, "Two Model Cities," p. 1.

Incentives, Political Education, and Behavior

Political arenas are not merely empty spaces in which competition for scarce resources takes place. Rather, arenas provide a structure of incentives which has an influence on the kinds of political behavior that will take place within them. And each individual actor need not scan and test the incentive structure himself; through a cumulative process of political education, he can learn from his associates which kinds of behavior are rewarded and which kinds are not.

In the electoral arena, success is achieved by building a majority coalition within a district or, in the case of city-wide offices, within the city at large. There is an incentive to build as inclusive a base of support as possible, by appealing publicly to groups on the basis of shared interests. In a city that does not have a black majority, black politicians' ability to determine city-wide policy will require active cooperation with whites who share their goals.

The electoral arena's incentives for building an inclusive coalition force a group to examine its own priorities in relation to those of other groups. A group may have to give in on some points, but in return it can win a share in controlling governmental decisions. As groups work together in a campaign to hammer out platform and strategy, a process of political education takes place. Stereotypes tend to break down in the working relationships that develop. And the results on election day show whether the majority building exercise has been successful.

If a political actor is successful in the campaign, then the backing of his constituency and his vote as a councilman provide him with a basis for bargaining with other elected leaders. With something to trade, he can then demand benefits for his constituency; agreements must be reached for any programs to go through. And if a combined slate has been successful in gaining control of a city council, then that slate can enact its joint program. Electoral cooperation can pay off in the opportunity to direct city policy.

The federal poverty program arena provides no comparable incentives for building a constituency in the community and then expanding that constituency by directing appeals to diverse groups. Rather than concentrating on forming a majority coalition in the city, a poverty program leader must pay attention to three narrower constituencies: the federal bureaucrats who fund his program, the local staff members and community organizers who operate the program, and those people who become involved in poverty neighborhood councils.

A poverty leader must prove to each of these groups that he is sufficiently "representative" of the poor. Federal administrators have constantly worried that the poverty leaders they fund will turn out not to be the "real" leaders of the poor or black community. Thus, there is the emphasis on finding people who are truly "representative." And, for these officials, an important indicator of representativeness is the militancy of rhetoric employed. If he is to prove himself representative, therefore, a poverty leader must utilize appeals that are more strident and more narrowly directed than successful electoral appeals would be. He must voice the frustrations of the poor, not produce a set of solutions which might prove acceptable to a wide range of groups. (The position of such a leader may be a tenuous one, for he is vulnerable to attack by those who utilize even more extreme rhetoric and tactics—and thus may appear to be even more "representative.")

In contrast to the electoral arena, the federal program arena offers little incentive for a political actor to expand his constituency and his audience. To do so, he would have to modify his appeal, which might make him appear to be less truly representative of the poor. Participants in the electoral arena must go beyond the question of each others' representativeness to try to forge agreement on specific policies and build a vehicle for achieving victory. If a person is considered to be representative, but he cannot bring votes to the ticket, then his usefulness in a campaign is doubtful.

While the electoral arena puts a high premium on cooperation between groups, the poverty program arena encourages separation by class and race. Separatism need not be opposed simply on the grounds that racial integration is preferable. Rather, it must be asked whether the policy values of the black community can best be served by a politics of separation. If economic redistribution is a prime goal of black political actors, and if the economic resources of middle and upper class whites are necessary to provide benefits to poor and black people, then separatism is a poor prescription for policy. (As better-off whites leave the cities for the suburbs, some sort of regional mechanism will have to be devised to effect meaningful redistribution. The maintenance of separate political arenas for poor people might make it easier for suburbanites to isolate themselve from demands for low-cost housing, jobs, and financial assistance to the city.)

Control Over What?

Not only do the arenas differ in the kinds of behavior they encourage; they also differ in the amounts and types of resources they contain. Although the federal program arena has provided funds for compensatory social services and organization for the poor, control of city government includes the potential for making decisions regarding city taxation, exercise of police power, hiring, firing, purchasing, licensing, and zoning in all areas of the city. Personnel practices and city services can be directed in ways which can redistribute benefits to those who presently lack them.[20] And, although Oakland's present political officials have not chosen to do so, city councilmen *can* use their power of appointment to influence the actions of both the city manager and autonomous commissioners.

Permanence and Independence

The two arenas also differ fundamentally in the bases upon which they rest. Federal programs, however bold their design and generous their appropriation, are subject to changes whenever an administration in Washington changes its mind. Thus, President Nixon announced in his proposed budget for fiscal year 1974 that he was seeking the outright abolition of several federal social programs—including OEO's Community Action Program.[21] Community representatives who participate in the federal program arena may find that the federal reed is an uncertain one on which to lean. And even when the flow of money is maintained, local actors in this arena are still continuously dependent upon federal officials.

[20] See Samuel Lubell's discussion of the effect of Mayor Carl Stokes's administration on Cleveland blacks in *The Hidden Crisis in American Politics* (New York: W. W. Norton, 1970), pp. 116-122.

[21] See *The New York Times*, January 30, 1973.

Success in the electoral arena, on the other hand, provides a political leader with a position in city government which cannot be removed by the stroke of a pen at a higher level of government. The relative permanence and independence of an electoral base reduces the vulnerability of elected office holders to the vagaries of outside governmental forces.

Government and Counter-Government

Successful electoral activity not only provides a base (and protection) for local political actors which is unavailable in the federal program arena; it can also be a vehicle for mobilizing the resource of numbers against other resources, such as money or social standing or control of communications media. The lack of power on the part of elected officials may lead to more power for those who presently hold these other resources. In Oakland, the weakness of elected politicians has facilitated the creation of a challenging counter-government, one which has been more disposed to press for programs which directly aid the poor. But for those who advocate policies which will redistribute resources to poor people and minorities, it may not be wise to substitute a strong non-elective counter-government for a strong elective government in a preferred model of urban politics. For there are other potential non-elective counter-governments in cities besides poverty organizations: business, labor, and newspapers, for example. If a city's electoral arena is ignored and its government is weak, then poor people—who might be expected to use their resource of numbers—can lose opportunities for action. Counter-governments are not a satisfactory substitute for the electoral process.

Two Arenas and Two Political Maladies

Although there appear to be a number of long-term advantages (control over city resources, independence, permanence, opportunity for utilizing the resource of numbers) in directing efforts toward the electoral arena, I do not mean to suggest that all of Oakland's black political leaders should immediately stop participating in federal programs and should start running for local office. For Oakland's governmental and political systems have made the electoral alternative an unattractive one at the present time. Low council salaries ($3,600) and the absence of strong electorally oriented groups make the strategy of municipal electoral politics an extremely risky one for a black political actor. Furthermore, at-large elections for each council seat make the process of majority building more difficult and expensive for electoral challengers.

In Oakland, the two arenas have suffered from different kinds of political maladies. Although the federal program arena, through the creation of numerous community groups, has stimulated a demand for policy results, the programs themselves have been subjected to uncertain funding and cannot produce the dramatic outcomes that might be expected from programs designed to "end poverty." This situation contrasts with that of the city's electoral arena, in which effective demand has been kept at a low level by the lack of active, strong groups and parties and by the inhospitable electoral rules. Although the city government does have a range of potential political resources (mostly unused by present incumbents), those who might want to exploit these resources most aggressively have not been able to secure them.

Warren Ilchman and Norman Uphoff[22] analyze such political maladies in terms of a political economy model. These authors focus on the ways in which various actors invest and exchange scarce resources in the political system. They describe a situation in which demand for political resources exceeds supply as "political inflation."[23] By contrast, "political deflation" occurs when the supply of resources exceeds demand. In this case, "authority is judged to be either too ineffective or too expensive relative to the costs of securing it and the benefits sought from it."[24] The Oakland poverty arena is a good example of "political inflation," while the city's electoral arena is in a state of "political deflation." In the former site of political activity, demand has been encouraged while supply has not been adequately provided. And in the latter site, demand has

[22] *The Political Economy of Change* (Berkeley and Los Angeles: University of California Press, 1969).
[23] *Ibid.*, p. 140.
[24] *Ibid.*, p. 145.

been discouraged by the high costs of electoral activity in a city lacking parties and election-oriented groups.

The recurring behavior patterns in each of Oakland's arenas have tended to reinforce those in the other and have also helped to maintain the gap between political demands and local government resources. Militant rhetoric in the poverty arena has increased city officials' already pronounced tendency to withdraw from the turbulent field of social programs, and inaction on the part of these officials has in turn led poverty activists to escalate their criticism of city government. Needing an enemy against whom to mobilize, actors in the federal program arena have repeatedly denounced Mayor Reading. And the mayor, viewing public controversy from the perspective of a private man, has tended to take these attacks personally. Knowing that he does not possess the powers his critics impute to him, and not understanding the role of exaggerated rhetoric in the new arena, Reading has usually responded to controversy by withdrawal.

Thus, more strident demands in the federal poverty arena have led to greater attempts by city officials to isolate themselves from those demands. Given these circumstances, separate arenas begin to resemble walled camps. And communication between them consists of debating and stereotyping, rather than bargaining over substantive policies.

Moving From Federal Programs to Electoral Politics

One arena (federal programs) has stimulated citizen participation but lacks a continuing and stable resource supply. Another arena (electoral politics) has the potential for providing a political base and redirecting certain city policies, but that arena has not been effectively entered by those who have participated in the first arena. Even though the city's electoral arena does not now appear to be an inviting option for poor and black people, the potential advantages of that arena make it worth inquiring to what degree links might be built from federal programs to electoral politics.

Indeed, it is sometimes suggested that federal programs are not substitutes for electoral politics; rather, by providing organizational resources and training, such programs prepare political actors for successful competition in the electoral arena. According to this view, federal programs are a first stage of political activity, and the control of city government is a second stage. But, as the next section will show, movement from one arena to another is by no means automatic, and the obstacles to building links between them are considerable.

THE DIFFICULTY OF BUILDING LINKS BETWEEN ARENAS

It is true that the skills required in each arena are not mutually exclusive; a person may attempt to use the organizing ability and community contacts which he developed in the federal program arena to mount a campaign for public office. But federal programs and city elections represent alternative targets for participation by local political actors, and time that is spent organizing and administering a poverty program cannot be spent registering voters or building a city-wide party organization. Besides, the patterns of behavior that have been encouraged in the poverty program arena are not those that are likely to lead to electoral success. The kind of uncompromising rhetoric employed by poverty leaders is unlikely to appeal to the diverse groups whose support is necessary for the building of a majority coalition.

A further obstacle to forging links between the federal program and electoral arenas may be provided by the structure of a city's political system. If that system does not contain politically active groups and party organizations which can be used to reach and mobilize voters, then movement into the electoral arena becomes much harder. The difficulty of building links between arenas, given a lack of viable electoral organizations, was clearly illustrated by the outcomes of recent election campaigns in Oakland.

During 1970 and 1971 a liberal, anti-incumbent coalition was formed to run a slate of candidates in the 1971 city council and school board elections. The coalition leaders consisted mostly of Democratic Party activists (who had previously concentrated on state and national campaigns but had been encouraged by recent liberal victories in the area to try to mount a municipal campaign) and some present and former participants in the federal program arena. Co-chairmen of this "Oakland Coalition" were John George, a black attorney who had serve on the OEDCI council and had also played a leading role in Democratic Party affairs; Bill Cavala, a University of California graduate student and manager of various Democratic campaigns in the area; Jack Aikawa, a leader in the Japanese-American community; and Mary Gay Thomas, representing Mexican-Americans.

The coalition's candidates, chosen at an open convention in January 1971, advocated actions by the city council which would increase the proportion of minorities hired by the city, provide incentives for policemen to live within Oakland's boundaries, preserve neighborhoods from commercial exploitation, and open council decisions to wider public participation. Furthermore, they suggested changes in the charter that would increase the authority of elected officials. Coalition-endorsed candidates, like coalition leaders, included people who had been active in the federal program arena. For example, Paul Cobb, who had been a central figure in both the poverty and model cities programs, was the coalition's nominee for the West Oakland council seat. But poverty activists were by no means agreed on their approach to the election. After OEDCI Executive Director Percy Moore announced on February 24 that he, with the aid of OEDCI staff, would ignore federal guidelines and launch an electoral campaign against incumbent councilmen, he endorsed some of the coalition nominees but supported different candidates for two council seats. Those coalition candidates who were endorsed by Moore refused his support, on the grounds that his actions were improper and were imperiling the future of the poverty program in Oakland.[25] Thus, various federal program activists battled with each other, as well as with the incumbents, in the electoral arena. Building a link from one arena to another was thus complicated by divisions among the challenging groups.

The difficulty of forging this link, as well as the continuing problems of organizing a compaign in a nongroup, nonparty environment, was demonstrated by the results. As Table 10 shows, incumbents were victorious in the April 20 elections.

[25] See *Oakland Tribune*, March 14, 1971.

Table 10: Incumbents Are Victorious in Oakland City Elections, April 1971

	Number of votes
Councilman	
District 1	
Felix Chialvo (Incumbent).........................	44,805
Betty Ann Bruno (Oakland Coalition)...............	42,658
District 3	
Dr. Raymond L. Eng (Incumbent)..................	48,467
Paul L. Cobb (Coalition)	36,120
Curtis Lee Baker	3,012
District 5	
Fred Maggiora (Incumbent)	50,893
Antonio Rodarte (Supported by Percy Moore).........	25,037
Dr. Kenneth Hoh (Write in; Coalition)..............	6,469
Lula M. Albert (Write in).........................	59
District 7	
Frank H. Ogawa (Incumbent)......................	49,474
Doug Jones (Coalition)............................	36,774
At-large	
Harvey Binns (Incumbent)	32,617
John Sutter (Coalition)	16,766
Stephen V. Brooks (Supported by Percy Moore).......	16,022
Rev. Frank Pinkard, Jr. (Coalition)	10,046
Jack Summerfield	5,045
Josephine M. Jimenez	2,000
Booker T. Emery.................................	1,255
Tito A. Lucero	1,087
Charles G. Murphy	569
School Director	
No. 1	
Barney E. Hilburn (Incumbent)	67,143
No. 2	
Mel J. Caughell (Incumbent).......................	53,455
Florencio Medina	26,644
No. 3	
Ann Root Corneille (Incumbent)	51,953
Jesse C. Guiterrez (Coalition)......................	28,744
No. 4	
Ellison W. Brown, Jr. (Coalition)...................	34,348
David S. Tucker, Jr...............................	30,363
Richard L. Doughty	15,979

Although the Oakland Coalition's multiracial slate (four blacks, one white, one Mexican-American, one Chinese-American, one Polynesian) won heavy majorities in the West and East Oakland ghettoes, they ran poorly in the rest of the city.[26] The coalition was continually hampered by a lack of funds and a shortage of personnel for precinct walking; with few political groups on which the campaign could rely, the going was rough indeed. Without vehicles for raising money and reaching voters with campaign messages, movement into the electoral arena was hindered.

The coalition did win one of the two runoff contests which resulted from the inability of any candidate to gain a clear majority on the first round. John Sutter, a prominent environmentalist and the only white candidate endorsed by the coalition, defeated conservative incumbent Harvey Binns by 37,500 to 34,990. But the coalition's candidate for the school board, Ellison Brown, a black member of the OEDCI council, lost to Republican David Tucker by a vote of 36,925 to 32,220. By concentrating their financial and organizational efforts on one council seat, Sutter supporters were able to win an upset victory over an incumbent. Still, for the coalition's black candidates, there had been no victories. (The council runoff had once again brought out divisions among the city's black leaders, as Percy Moore and his associates defied the Oakland Coalition by supporting Binns against Sutter.)

Oakland's political environment and electoral rules (Paul Cobb won in his district but lost the at-large election) had combined with internal divisions to show clearly that a move from the federal program arena to the electoral arena is a difficult one to make in that city.[27] The challengers had achieved one victory, but they had also learned that electoral success requires long-term participation. Election-oriented organiza-

[26] See *ibid.*, April 25, 1971.

[27] A possible parallel might be made to the problem of infant industries in developing countries. These industries, which have been nurtured under tariff-protected conditions, have had difficulty in moving into successful competition in an unprotected economy. See Gerald M. Meier, *International Trade and Development* (New York: Harper and Row, 1963), pp. 124-127. I would like to thank Professor Frank S. Levy for suggesting this analogy to me.

tions have to be built, and attempts must be made to expand constituencies and build coalitions. If links are to be built between the two arenas, then sustained electoral effort over time is needed.

The difficulties of electoral organizing in Oakland were demonstrated again in the 1973 mayoral campaign. Once again, there was fragmentation of effort on the part of those seeking to unseat the incumbent. Three Democratic candidates—two of them black—waged an intense and often bitter campaign for similar constituencies in the election's first round. In the runoff (Mayor Reading having missed an outright majority by 54 votes in the first round), the mayor defeated ex-Black Panther activist Bobby Seale by 77,476 (64 percent) to 43,719 (36 percent).[28] Although Seale did considerably better than most observers had initially predicted, the challengers to Oakland's *status quo* were still a long way from electing a mayor. The lack of party mechanisms—which might have been able to build consensus behind an endorsed candidate—had allowed three different campaigns to battle for the liberal constituency, and in the runoff active supporters of the other Democratic candidates gave little help to Seale. The absence of strong electoral groups in Oakland had again proved to be an obstacle to those seeking governmental change.

Some Concluding Observations

Although federal poverty and employment funds created a separate arena for political action in Oakland, in which competition for jobs, money, and authority could take place, such an arena cannot be regarded as a substitute for the city's electoral arena. For there are important differences between the arenas in the kinds of behavior encouraged, the amounts and types of resources available, and the permanence of the arenas themselves. Because electoral success can result in controlling the direction of a range of city policies, participants in the federal program arena might well wish to enter the electoral arena. But their ability to do so may be limited by a number of factors: the difficulty of spending time in both

[28] See "Reading Defeats Seale easily for Oakland Mayor," *The New York Times*, May 17, 1973.

poverty programs and electoral politics; the negative effect of militant rhetoric in building majority coalitions; and the lack of viable electoral groups through which to mount a campaign.

By creating programs which reward certain kinds of action, federal officials can have an important effect on the behavior of local political actors. If separate poverty programs are funded and City Hall is bypassed, then the incentives for blacks to enter the electoral arena are reduced. One way to encourage increased electoral participation might be to make city government the recipient of federal social programs. But this strategy would not be an appealing one if the incumbents of City Hall were not responsive to the needs of poor people and minorities. The problem (to which I will return in the last chapter) is to devise ways of strengthening elected officials in the long run, while ensuring that the needs of disadvantaged people are met.

Although federal officials, through their funding decisions, can have an impact on a city's politics, the nature of that impact is strongly influenced by the characteristics of the local political system itself. Thus, conflict avoidance, denial of their own authority, and underutilization of resources on the part of Oakland's elected officials made possible the creation of a separate arena which was hostile to City Hall. And the amorphous, nongroup nature of the Oakland political system made movement from the federal program arena to the electoral arena extremely difficult. Policy outcomes reflect both federal designs and local political realities.

4

Images:
Federal and Local Officials View Each Other

In the last chapter, I examined the effect of particular federal programs on local politics and the effect of local political behavior on federal program outcomes. Now I will turn to an analysis of bargaining between federal and local officials. Such bargaining does not take place in a vacuum; the way federal and local actors behave with respect to each other is conditioned both by their images of each other and by their organizational objectives in the aid process itself. In this chapter, I will focus on federal and local officials' perceptions of each other. And in the next chapter, I will show how these actors respond to the organizational problems involved in the aid process.

IMAGES IN INTERORGANIZATIONAL RELATIONS

Participants in federal-city negotiations are not disengaged individuals; they belong to organizations whose members hold certain shared images of the world around them. In this essay, one group's "image" of another is defined as its perception of the other's basic characteristics and motivations. Such images are useful for dealing with the environment in which these organizations operate. Anthony Downs has listed the following general conditions of the bureaucratic environment:

Information is costly because it takes time, effort, and sometimes money to obtain data and comprehend their meaning.
—Decision-makers have only limited capabilities regarding the amount of time they can spend making decisions, the number of issues they can consider simultaneously, and the amount of data they can absorb regarding any one problem.
—Although some uncertainty can be eliminated by acquiring information an important degree of ineradicable uncertainty is usually involved in making decisions.[1]

Because of these limitations on their time, information, and cognitive capacity, organizational actors use images to simplify their environments. Shared images of the world provide a way for members of an organization to evaluate and deal with outside groups without expending scarce resources to gain extensive information about them.

A number of social scientists have discussed the importance of images in the context of international relations. Robert Jervis has stated: "In determining how he will behave, an actor must try to predict how others will act and how their actions will affect his values. The actor must therefore develop an image of others and of their intentions."[2] Drawing on both psychological and historical evidence, Jervis puts forward the hypothesis that "decision-makers tend to fit incoming information into their existing theories and images. Indeed, their theories and images play a large part in determining what they notice."[3]

Graham T. Allison and Morton H. Halperin, in presenting their "bureaucratic politics" approach to international relations, also point to the important role played by images in shaping the thinking of foreign policy makers: "Perceptions of issues or arguments about the national interest do not begin *ab initio*. Beneath the differences that fuel bureaucratic politics is a foundation of shared assumptions about basic values and

[1] Anthony Downs, *Inside Bureaucracy* (Boston: Little, Brown, 1967), p. 3.
[2] Robert Jervis, "Hypotheses on Misperception," *World Politics* 20 (April 1968), p. 454.
[3] *Ibid.*, p. 455.

facts. These underlying assumptions are reflected in various attitudes and images which are taken for granted by most players."[4] According to the authors, these shared images are resistant to change and are reinforced by the behavior of members of the organization:

> Most participants tend to interpret the actions of other nations to make them consistent with held images, rather than reexamining basic views. Even those in the bureaucracy who do not share some or all of these values and images are inclined to argue as if they believed them. They do this because to do otherwise would make them suspect by other members of the bureaucracy.[5]

In domestic intergovernmental relations also, local and federal organizations have developed images of each other which influence the perceptions of individuals within those organizations. In order to learn how local and federal officials viewed each other, I conducted interviews in the summer of 1972 with twelve federal officials with responsibility for programs in Oakland and with eleven Oakland city officials who were charged with negotiating with federal agencies.[6] The interviews averaged one-and-a-half to two hours in length, and focused on the way in which the "feds" viewed the locals, or vice versa.

Images are useful aids to intergovernmental actors in gaining a grip on their environment, because reliable information about the other level of government is difficult to come by. A federal official observed that city governments "are hard to figure." And a number of local officials spoke of federal procedures as "a mess" that they had difficulty in understanding. For a federal actor with responsibility for administering programs in a number of localities, it would be extremely time-consuming to gather and carefully analyze information on the diverse political systems in those localities. Furthermore, potential sources of helpful information are not easy to identify. And local actors, hard-pressed for time and financial resources, are not in a position to inform themselves in depth about the multiplicity

---

[4] Graham T. Allison and Morton H. Halperin, "Bureaucratic Politics: A Paradigm and Some Policy Implications," *World Politics* 24 (Spring 1972), p. 56.

[5] *Ibid.*

[6] Federal agencies represented were: HEW; HUD; Department of Labor; OEO. Local officials were from the following departments: Mayor's Office; City Council; City Manager's Office; City Manpower Department; City Attorney's Office; City Planning Department; Redevelopment Agency; City Poverty Program.

of federal agencies with whom they deal. Even if they had more time and money, the problem of finding reliable sources of information would not disappear.

Both federal and local representatives were able to list some ways in which they could find out about the other level of government. Federal officials mentioned: reading local newspapers, examining the reports of local program operators, talking to other federal representatives, walking the streets, going to local churches, and collecting rumors. Local officials said that they relied upon conversations with federal representatives to learn about federal policy. But both sets of officials observed that it was not easy for them to find out about the other. One federal representative explained how she learned about a city's politics, given the lack of consistently reliable information: "It's basically filtering gossip and putting it together. When there are divergences, I figure the truth is somewhere in between." Faced with the difficulty of obtaining information about particular programs, cases, and individuals, federal and local actors make use of general images of the other side. These mental pictures, which provide clues as to the likely actions of others, are used by an intergovernmental actor in deciding what positions he himself will take.

In the following discussion, I will first spell out the feds' and locals' images of each other, based on repeated themes which emerged from the interviews. Then I will show how these images affect the interaction between officials and how they influence the negotiating positions officials on each side take.

FEDS' VIEW OF LOCALS

1. *City officials don't see the whole picture.*—Federal officials argue that local governments are too close to problems to see the interrelationships among them. In designing policies, they say, the locals take too narrow an approach. Speaking of the locals' outlook, a federal program director observed: "They all have some concern about community development, but we find it difficult to articulate to them the range of activities under community development and how these activities must relate

with each other to get the best mileage for the buck." According to this federal representative, the locals' narrow view sometimes makes it frustrating to deal with them: "It is difficult sometimes to get through to the city one of the basic philosophies of physics—for every action there is a reaction. You can't go and plan a redevelopment project without setting up housing resources. We talk in these terms to them; but constantly we find that it doesn't sink in."

Part of this narrowness, the feds explain, comes from being too close to the ground to take an over-arching view. But another part of it comes from a desire on the part of local officials to protect their own organizational position. As a federal representative remarked: "Coordination, to a lot of local officials, is an attempt to take away whatever power they might think they have." For a variety of reasons, then, the feds feel that locals do not take a broad enough view of problems and policies in their cities. (Indeed, the assertion of their own ability to take the larger view is a prime ingredient in the feds' rationale for intervention in local affairs.)

2. *City officials are interested in federal money, but they're not really interested in programs.*—Federal officials see their local counterparts as desiring infusions of federal dollars. A federal project operator declared: "Every city official I've talked to is concerned with money—the more the better. The only limiting factor is the tax rate—they can't come up with the local share." But a desire for federal dollars is not, federal officials say, necessarily linked to enthusiasm for operating programs and solving problems. "As a rule," said one federal representative, "I don't think that city managers and *certainly* city councils are interested in problem-solving. But they want money and they don't want to take the heat of raising it themselves."

The reasons given by feds for locals' reluctance to get involved in federal programs are numerous:

—Our programs are not under their control.
—The city likes to deal with things and products, rather than programs. They'll do an eyeglass program or a recreation program, but as far as devising projects to attack poverty, they're not as good.
—City officials are cautious and budget-minded.
—Racial considerations have infected the power structure of city hall.

When local officials do participate in such programs, say the feds, they do so without vision or enthusiasm. Local officials are seen as concentrating on the details of a program, rather than on its overall goals. As one federal man observed: "The City Council is concerned with the proper expenditure of funds. They question the improper expenditure of funds. They are less concerned with programmatic things. Rather, they'll ask: 'Is it legal to use the money to go to lunches?' and things like that."

If local officials have uneasy feelings about federal programs, why don't they just give them up? According to the feds, locals know that this is not "politically feasible." A federal representative explained:

> It's a double-edged kind of thing. To them [local officials] a lot of federal programs are a pain. In many cases, they'd rather not bother. But they can't afford to drop. For example, the Oakland City Council bitched and moaned about matching for the Emergency Employment Act. They looked upon this as a new chore. Still, they couldn't afford to turn it down because of the political consequences.

An operator of a social program spelled out some of these political consequences in explaining why Oakland could not afford to drop her program: "They had no choice, politically. There is a huge black constituency in Oakland—Oakland will be ripe for a black mayor. So they can't ignore it politically. The city is shifting to the Democrats."

3. *City governments are constrained—and sometimes like to be constrained—by local bureaucratic procedures.*—Federal officials were unanimous in complaining about city "bureaucracy" and city "red tape." According to the feds, convoluted city procedures cause unnecessary and painful delay in the administration of programs. For example, a federal representative commented that:

> The problems are continuous. It is very difficult for a city government that's set up for city business to be in the [federal program] business. They wanted to treat this program as city business and make every request go through numerous city departments. Each desk it had to go through had peculiar kinds of guidelines, and it had to go through ten different desks. Nothing was *moving*.

According to the feds, cities are hamstrung by stringent charter provisions, civil service rules, purchasing regulations, and widespread institutional fragmentation. City officials were often not to blame for delay, the feds argued, because they were at the mercy of constraining procedures.

Other federal actors, while admitting that city procedures caused problems for local officials, expressed the view that the locals were using these procedures as excuses for avoiding action they would prefer to avoid anyway. For example, one federal program manager remarked: "The city manager said he wasn't sure the City Council would accept presale housing inspection. He uses the Council as a reason not to do things." Another interviewee provided a similar observation: "City attorneys are conservative protectors of the old line. Most city attorneys are over 50, and well-entrenched in city government. They just cite thing after thing explaining why they can't do the things you want them to do." Still another federal representative talked about the locals' practice of constraining themselves through the city charter: "One of their favorite arguments is 'We can't do that—it conflicts with the city charter.' So I say: 'Why not change the city charter?' And they say no. It's just like asking them to burn the Bible." (Not surprisingly, federal officials took a somewhat more reverent view of their own statutes and administrative guidelines.)

The image of locals as constraint-seekers was underscored by a federal program operator who recounted this dialogue with a local official:

Local: Mr. ——-, what does [federal department] think on this?
Fed: It's a matter of local option.
Local: But what does [federal department] think?
Fed: Local option.
Local: I want to know what [federal department] wants to do.
Fed: Well, I can't tell you.

The teller of the story pictured the local official as searching for an external federal constraint in the absence of an internal one. "Even if we get them to make the decision themselves," the federal actor remarked, "they often blame it on us. 'Oh, the Department of ——- *told* us to do it.'"

4. *City officials respond to local political consider-*

ations—specifically, to the local "establishment"—rather than to the public interest.—When asked to give her impressions of local officials, a federal program manager responded: "Local officials are interested in their own political advancement. That's the only common denominator." Federal officials frequently said that local decisions were taken in response to "political" considerations.

According to the feds, local officials are political in a number of different ways. First of all, local elected officials aim squarely —sometimes exclusively—at the goal of reelection. As one federal representative put it: "They don't really care about solving the problems of the poor. They're interested in whether they're going to get reelected. It's kind of curious. . . . They want that job so bad—and then they don't do anything with it." After elections, said another federal actor, the locals reward those who voted for them: "The City Council always responds to pressure from its own constituents. The Council responds to organizations that helped to elect them—special interest organizations. People support people and then expect payoffs." The federal official referred to this practice as part of the "rip-off syndrome."

Feds also spoke of locals as acting "politically" in their subservience to the dominant political group—or "establishment"—in their community. Consider this comment by a federal official: "Local officials are not interested really in the program or its potential but the threatening aspect of it to the prevailing view of community leaders. That's the establishment, but I try to avoid that term." These dominant groups, say the feds, use money to gain governmental access. As one federal staff member remarked: "Nobody who doesn't have money can penetrate a city attorney's office."

Finally, federal officials see locals as practicing political decision-making when they choose on the basis of narrow private interests, rather than a broader public interest. In the view of a program manager: "Politics are often injected into our program at the local level. Some neighborhood group would get the mayor's ear, get hold of a [federal department] booklet, and get a neighborhood facility put in. But that was not necessarily where a neighborhood facility was needed."

This political outlook, say federal actors, contributes to the narrow view of local officials. Concentrating on political pressures, they can easily lose sight of larger objectives: "Take the City Council members, the concerns they have, the pressures they're worried about. Can we get it through without causing any problems? Can we get it through [federal agency]? Can we get it through without causing a political stink? Can we get it by the auditor?"

In contrast, feds see themselves as thinking about a larger "public interest." A federal representative, in arguing against revenue-sharing, advanced the view that "the further down you get in the structure, the less chance you have of making a decision free of political influence." In this view, the focus of locals is not only narrow; it is tied to the preferences of powerful special interests. The feds see themselves as sufficiently disengaged from local politics to have a more balanced and systemic perspective.

In summary, feds see locals as: unable to view the interrelationships among problems and among programs, interested in federal money but not in the purposes of federal programs, constrained by bureaucratic procedures and institutional fragmentation, and responding to political pressures at the local level.

This is not to argue that all federal bureaucrats share the same view of all local officials. For one thing, there are differences from one agency to another. Representatives of OEO were more likely to see cities as dominated by an "establishment" than were members of the Department of Labor. Furthermore, federal officials sometimes drew distinctions between types of local officials. For example, they tended to view city administrators as being more knowledgeable than city councilmen. As I shall emphasize in the next chapter, federal and local officials do not face each other as two monolithic blocs. Nevertheless, in the course of the interviews, certain common themes were frequently expressed by federal officials in describing their local counterparts—and by locals in describing feds. It is my purpose here to present these common themes and to examine some of their implications.

LOCALS' VIEW OF FEDS

1. *Federal officials are too far away to understand a city's problems or politics.* —Expressing sentiments that were shared by many of his local colleagues, a city councilman remarked: "We're closer to our constituents than federal people are. They're way up there in Washington. We have this direct contact that makes us more aware." A local program director saw the feds' geographical distance from local problems as supplemented by a kind of mental detachment: "Federal officials have sort of a zen-like approach to things: detached non-attachment. They're sort of detached." In contrast, he observed that "city officials are much more concerned with day-to-day things that are happening around them."

According to the locals, the feds' distance from a city means that they cannot gain an understanding of that city's unique problems. One local executive remarked that "local officials have a greater knowledge and a deeper knowledge of what should be done in a given area. Every locality has a unique labor situation. It's difficult for someone in Washington who is not familiar with it to talk about the type of training and extent of training that is needed for local industries."

Not only were the distant feds felt to be out of touch with local substantive problems; they were also described by local officials as lacking understanding of the complexities of city politics. A local program director observed:

> The feds ... are totally naive about local politics and the important role it plays in citizen involvement. ... Unless you're aware of the delicate relationship between the mayor and the city manager, one having authority and the other the ability to be persuasive, then you get a gap between lines of authority. Feds are very removed from day-to-day problems of cities. They're just too far away.

2. *Feds are spenders.*—A veteran local oficial observed that "the feds are concerned that the money is spent at a proper rate. This is a shift—to a concern with spending money. This is a reversal of roles for us; we're normally concerned with saving money." Another local executive expanded on this

theme, contrasting federal and local attitudes toward spending: "It's a whole shift of philosophy for our more traditional guys. As you know, we have a severe financial crisis in the city. We've had to watch every dime. Now along comes a federal agency and says [spend]—you're not spending enough, you're not spending fast enough. It's a real clash of philosophies."

An exasperated city councilman, to whom the federal government often appeared to be giving away money for no particular purpose, registered his opposition: "Money should not be given out—it should be creative. In private business, you don't dole out money just to dole it out. You might give it away for tax deductions, but the government doesn't need tax deductions." In contrast to their high-spending federal counterparts, locals see themselves as people who know the value of a dollar and the importance of thrift.

3. *Federal officials are naive—not practical enough.*—In the eyes of local officials, the feds are unrealistically optimistic about the ease with which urban problems can be solved. A cause of this naiveté, according to one local administrator, is the fact that "the feds are not up against the brunt of dealing with people." Locals feel that the feds make demands on them which ignore the difficulty of training people and working with people: "They insist on the one hand on more minority participation. But there just aren't people in minority areas with enough experience." And local officials cited federal projects in the city in which participating citizens had made "silly" or "unreasonable" requests: "There were the senior citizens' projects. They made a request for a trip to Reno—for the obvious reasons. We had to turn them down. They said: 'Travel is broadening.' "

Local officials also see the feds as being naively optimistic about the workings of their own programs—imagining "linkages" and "coordination" and "progress" where none of these things exist. In the words of a long-time city administrator: "The feds keep talking about linkages, which is crap. We get tired of fights between federal departments—Labor and OEO or HUD and OEO. There's employment money in Labor, employment money in OEO, employment money in HUD. They're talking about linkages—coordination so that there's a minimum of duplication. A lot of wheel spinning goes into 'coordination' instead of carrying out the program."

Finally, locals see feds as being overly optimistic about the city's capacity to carry out federal designs. "Most federal programs don't take into consideration the reality of cities that they're in. Look at our public housing administration, what they've done. Look at redevelopment. They don't take into account the realities of what a city can do and can't do—the monies a city has to spend."

Because feds are naive about the solubility of urban problems and the capacities of government, say the locals, they are inclined to rush into projects too quickly. Federal program administrators are criticized for not understanding that proper procedures take time. In contrast, city officials see themselves as being more practical, businesslike, and aware of the complexities of life. "If the city had its way," said one veteran local administrator, "we'd be more concerned with physical projects. A lot of those [federal] programs are silly." (Of course, from the locals' viewpoint, having the feds identified with social programs has its advantages; the federal government is a convenient scapegoat for the difficulties that befall such programs.)

4. *Feds are two faced; they rush into programs and then hold the locals responsible for their proper administration.*— Local officials see the feds as telling them one story in the program inception period and a very different story in the follow-through phase. City administrators often complained about federal financial commitments which were reneged upon. (The phenomena of donor overpromises and recipient unfulfilled expectations will be treated in the next chapter, as part of a discussion of organizational problems in the aid process.) Even when funding did come through, local officials complained that shifts in federal emphasis created problems at the local level. Speaking of the follow-through phase of one program, a local representative recalled: "The [federal] auditors said we didn't have sufficient documentation for expenditures. Now, they didn't tell us that [earlier]. They said 'let's get the program on the road.' They didn't tell us to wait for these things."

With respect to the issue of citizen participation, locals had a similar perception of federal behavior: rush into a policy, but hold the local officials responsible for how it comes out. As a city administrator complained:

> The federal government gets you both ways. First, they tell you that you have to get more community participation. *Let* the citizens make mistakes, the federal agencies say. Let them open their own checking accounts, let them spend their money on anything they want. And then the GAO and the federal accountants turn around and hold you personally responsible for it. Now I wouldn't mind letting these people make mistakes if the city were not entirely responsible for it.

A number of city officials made it clear that it was often different federal officials who carried the different stories. "Program types" rushed into action, while "auditor types" checked up later. Thus, it might be said that it was the federal system, rather than an individual, that was "two-faced." Still, the suspicion remained that the program people ought to warn local officials about the actions that the auditors were going to take.

   5. *Federal officials are constrained—by legislation and by their own bureaucratic procedures.*—A number of local officials expressed the view that federal officials as individuals were reasonable, but that they were constrained by the structure and procedures of their own system. The blame was often placed on federal guidelines. In the words of a city councilman, "I'm sure that federal representatives understand our situation, except that their hands are tied with federal guidelines." This sentiment was echoed by another local official, who linked the guidelines to legislation: "As far as individuals we've dealt with, there's been nothing but cooperation. Any problems we've had result from legislation—the restrictions written into it." Still another local representative commented on the uncertainties of the federal legislative process: "House, Senate, all those compromises. What comes out? No bill will affect everyone equally."

   In the local view, the federal administrative structure provides another set of roadblocks to flexibility and direct action. Just as federal officials are seen as too far removed from cities to deal effectively with their problems, so the distances within federal bureaucracies themselves are perceived as huge. Even if a well-meaning federal bureaucrat wants to respond to the preferences of city officials, he will have difficulty in getting others in his organization to act accordingly.

Some local officials see the regional federal representatives as being sympathetic to the locals' needs, and the Washington people as being out of touch. As one city representative remarked:

> At one end of a scale, there's the guy who comes into this office and sits down and talks about a program. He has a pretty good idea of what cities need and want. But at the other end of the scale, there's the staff in Washington; they're developing policy based on second hand information. That causes distortions, or alterations at least, of what a city needs.

Others see the top federal officials as wanting to give the locals more power but being foiled by those lower down. Noting that "the top echelon of the administration may have a particular policy . . . which they subscribe to, but that approach may not be accepted by people further down," a local administrator said: "That's true of the Nixon administration. The top echelon wants to turn over responsibility to local government. But lower bureaucrats try to achieve their own social objectives with the muscle of their resources."

Although they differ in their identification of allies within the federal system, local officials are united in viewing the bureaucratic structure as large, convoluted, and confusing. One city representative summed it up nicely: "The federal government seems to me like a huge dragon. Even if there is a policy shift, it takes a long, long time for that shift to travel all the way down the tail to the lower bureaucrats."

Thus, to summarize, locals see feds as: too far away to grasp a city's problems; in a hurry to spend money; naively optimistic about the ease with which problems can be solved; two-faced, in that they rush into programs and then hold locals responsible for them; and constrained by legislation and bureaucracy.

Once again, there were differences in perception between one official and another. Those city representatives who had had extensive experience in dealing with federal programs were more likely to view federal officials favorably than were those who had not had such experience. And local officials did not

see the feds as an undifferentiated mass; they expressed more
resentment against OEO and HEW (whom they viewed as
sponsoring experimental social programs) than against other
departments (whom they saw as more interested in traditional
kinds of programs relating to physical structures and jobs.)

Still, as was the case with federal officials, there were certain
common components in the local officials' expressed images of
their counterparts at another level of government. Having seen
the feds' images of the locals and the locals' images of the feds,
let us now consider some of the implications of these images
for federal-local interactions.

THE IMAGE-HOLDERS MEET: FRICTION MODERATED BY AWARENESS OF CONSTRAINTS

Images as Sources of Strain

The images I have described are used by intergovernmental
actors to simplify a complex reality. And such simplification
can lead to friction. When, in the summer of 1972, Oakland's
city manager delayed in implementing a HUD request to create
a new position of assistant city manager for community development, federal officials considered the delay just another
example of the locals' narrowness and timidity. The manager's
office, which was trying to resolve city departmental controver-
sies regarding the title and powers of the new position, viewed
the feds' impatience as illustrating federal distance from and
ignorance of city governmental problems. Each side felt that
its true motives were not being understood by the other; federal
officials stressed that they just wanted to help the city plan
its community development activities, while local actors said
that they were trying to make sure the new position had support
within the city government.

Another case of reciprocal images contributing to strain
occurred when the city government made plans in 1972 to
transfer the local Head Start program from the Community
Action Agency (then linked to the city, but with a citizen
participation component) to the school system. Federal officials, concerned about preserving the program's links to the

black community, saw this as further proof of local subservience to dominant political interests, who were critical of community action programs. Local officials saw federal disapproval as another indication that feds were naive about social programs; the locals argued that practical people would realize that school professionals could run a children's program better than could a citizens' board. Once again, each side relied upon its dominant images of the other in assessing the situation. And once again, neither side believed that its true motives were being appreciated.

Not only do these reciprocal images have the potential to cause strain in the interaction of those who hold them; attempts by each side to "reform" the other may have the effect of reinforcing negative images and escalating hostility. If feds see locals as too narrow and cautious, they may try to move them more forcefully into programs—which only reinforces the locals' view that the feds are too inclined to rush into things. Similarly, if the locals see the feds as over-optimistic and naive, they may be cautious about entering into new federal programs— thus reinforcing the feds' image of them as being overly timid.

Hostility Moderated by Perceptions of Fragmentation

With respect to international relations, Jervis puts forward the hypotheses that: "there is an overall tendency for decision-makers to see other states as more hostile than they are"[7] and that "actors tend to see the behavior of others as more centralized, disciplined, and coordinated than it is."[8] We have seen that, in domestic intergovernmental relations, some of the images that federal and local actors hold of each other are unfavorable. But these views are not entirely hostile, and one important reason for this is that each set of actors does *not* see the other as "centralized, disciplined, and coordinated." Federal officials talk about the existence of numerous narrow, fragmented agencies at the local level. And city representatives note the divisions between federal agencies and between different parts of the same agency. We have seen that each side views the fragmentation of the other as a constraint on coor-

[7] Jervis, "Hypotheses on Misperception," p. 475.
[8] *Ibid.*

dinated and disciplined action. It may be argued that domestic policy actors, in contrast to those in international relations, are able to gain enough information about each other to recognize internal divisions on the other side. At any rate, the recognition of such divisions, and the belief that they are obstacles to quick action, lead federal and local actors to view each others' plight with some sympathy. It becomes possible to blame the governmental system, rather than an individual, for rigidity and delay.

Other Factors Reducing Hostility

Another force for the moderation of intergovernmental tension is the perception on both sides of certain occupational categories—lawyers, accountants, program operators, for example—which cut across governmental levels and which have their own views of the world. A lawyer on the city staff remarked: "The federal legal officers—with HUD, OEO, and Labor—tell me they have problems with *their* administrative people. And auditors are a world unto themselvs, the group with pads and pencils. They don't care about either administrative or legal questions." And a federal program manager, who remarked that city staffs tended to have "a core of at least two or three people who could adequately define problems," spoke of the existence of "unholy alliances between federal field staff and city staff which puts the local leadership in a position where they must address problems."

Taking an overview of the situation, a city staff man talked about the different orientations which exist within both federal and city levels:

> There is a program-auditor dichotomy. And that exists at both levels. Program representatives don't care very much about the fine print— "Thou shalt keep the books in such and such a manner." Program types will go ahead with just about anything, and if you go ahead and do that, you get hit by an auditor type. It's a very common kind of problem. Program types get very frustrated and very antsy and view it as resistance. But I think it's mostly a different type of orientation.

Thus, lawyers, accountants, and "program types" among both feds and locals view themselves linked in orientation to people at the other level of government.

Still another factor reducing hostility is the existence of people whose jobs do not fall clearly into "federal" or "local" categories, but contain elements of both. One cross-pressured young man, who was a member of the city staff but funded by the federal government, remarked: "I don't think of myself as either a city official or a federal official." He saw the role of his office as presenting the city's point of view to the feds and explaining the federal program to city officials. In this way, such people can provide a link between the two levels.

Finally, there are perceptions of ties that bind public officials together. A city staff member offered the opinion that "the antagonisms between city and federal officials is less than between the citizenry and *any* official. There is a greater degree of cooperation and clubbiness between federal and city officials." One can see a recognition of shared, as well as opposing, interests between federal and local actors; intergovernmental participants do not see their relationship as being a zero-sum game.

The Problem of Playing Different Games

Although there are a number of elements in federal-local perceptions which help to moderate hostility, representatives of both sides report that negotiations between them are frequently strained. The existence of friction does not necessarily mean that federal and local actors are directly arguing about conflicting policy preferences; strain may also be caused by differences between the two sides in the identification of which issues are important. Jervis puts forward the hypothesis that it is very hard for one actor to see that issues which are important to him are not important to others. "While he may know that another actor is on an opposing team, it may be more difficult for him to realize that the other is playing an entirely different game. This is especially true when the game he is playing seems vital to him."[9]

Federal officials, with their emphasis on shaping broad policy with reference to numerous cities, and local officials, who are concerned with specific local pressures, may see the same policy in the context of two very different games. And this difference

9 *Ibid.*, p. 478.

in perspective can lead to friction even in the absence of substantive disagreement. In Oakland during 1972, federal and local officials did not argue over the merits of appointing or not appointing an assistant city manager for community development. The feds, who were concerned with increasing the capacity of city governments to coordinate diverse programs, became impatient with the city's delay. And the locals, who were preoccupied with keeping peace within the city bureaucracy, became irritated at the feds' prodding. Neither side disagreed with the creation of the new job, but the two groups of officials viewed the matter from the standpoint of different sets of concerns. Each side was operating in its own game, which it viewed as being worthy of the other side's attention.

IMPLICATIONS OF IMAGES FOR NEGOTIATING POSITIONS

The images that federal and local officials have of each other have certain implications for the kinds of requests that each side tends to make of the other in the negotiating process. For example, the feds' perception that locals view their problems too narrowly is reflected in federal demands that local governments engage in long-range comprehensive planning exercises. To take another example, the federal officials' view that their city counterparts are not sufficiently committed to federal programs leads to an insistence on local matching shares which represent new financial contributions, as opposed to the counting of existing spending. This, the feds argue, increases local commitment to a program. Finally, federal officials' perception of local political systems as being dominated by narrow "establishments" emerged from the interviews as a reason behind federal insistence on various forms of citizen participation in programs.

On the other side, the locals' view of the feds as being too far away to understand a city's problems leads to local leaders' insistence that program standards be flexible enough to take into account the situation of a particular city. Because of local officials' perception that the federal government has a tendency not to follow through on its promises, local representatives ask their federal counterparts for guarantees that projects which are started will be funded and completed. And because city officials see a communications gap between Washington feds and those in the field, they seek assurances from both groups that a program will have continuing support.

Thus, the sets of images that feds and locals have of each other play a part in shaping the positions taken in negotiations between the groups. And those negotiating positions can in turn lead to the process of reinforcing images which was discussed earlier. When federal officials, viewing Oakland city leaders as too closely tied to the local "establishment," pressed for more participation by black citizens in the poverty and model cities programs, local officials interpreted that position as further evidence of the feds' naiveté about social policies. And when the locals tried to "educate" their federal counterparts by stressing the difficulties of implementing such participation, the feds saw this reaction as further evidence of local narrowness. The use of images can simplify a complex environment, but it can also lead to friction in the negotiating process.

SUMMARY

Bargaining between federal and local officials is structured by the images that each side has of the other. Because of the limitations on their time, information, and cognitive capacities, intergovernmental actors use images to simplify their environment and to deal with other actors within that environment.

Federal actors see their local counterparts as too close to their own problems to take a sufficiently broad view of them, and as too constrained by bureaucratic and political pressures to act "in the public interest." The locals, on the other hand, see the feds as far removed from local problems, over-optimistic about solutions to those problems, and bound up by their own bureaucratic procedures.

Although these images are the sources of some hostility between federal and local actors, there are certain elements within the images which moderate that hostility. In particular, the perception of each side by the other as constrained by organizational fragmentation makes it possible to blame non-performance on the inadequacies of the system, rather than on those of the individuals within it.

Images have certain implications for the positions taken by federal and local actors in negotiations with each other. Federal officials, for example, who see the locals as too narrow in their focus, insist on long-range comprehensive planning in order to broaden that focus. And locals, who view the feds as too far away to understand their particular problems, insist on the right to tailor programs to fit their city. Thus, the images which are used by intergovernmental actors to make sense of their environment have an influence on the way those actors behave with respect to each other.

5
Donors, Recipients, and the Aid-Giving Process

Continuing our analysis of the interaction between federal and local officials, let us focus now on the dynamics of the aid relationship itself. For the actors under study are participants in a process of aid giving and receiving, and their behavior is in large measure a response to some of the organizational problems posed by that process. In this chapter, I will begin by presenting a general model of the aid process. Then I will show how interaction between the elements of that model produces difficulties for both donors and recipients and also generates conflict between these groups. Compounding donor-recipient tensions is a difference in perspective between those who formulate general policies and those who are charged with their local implementation. As I will demonstrate in the last section of this chapter, efforts to close the gap between aid givers and receivers have typically focused on creating a joint commitment to goals, rather than on building a framework for collaborative day-to-day actions.

Because foreign aid and federal urban aid programs are both manifestations of the aid-giving process, I will draw illustrations and examples from both experiences. Although foreign aid involves relations between two sovereign polities, while federal aid to cities involves relations between central and local governments within the same country, I have been struck by the parallels in organizational difficulties—and responses to them— found in these two programs. A perusal of literature on foreign aid[1] was helpful to me in both identifying and explaining some recurring dilemmas of aid participants in Oakland.

MODEL OF THE AID PROCESS

In an aid-giving situation, the donor provides grants or loans (or both) to a recipient. The following model will specify both underlying constraints on participants' behavior and the distinctive organizational objectives of the givers and receivers of assistance.

Some Basic Constraints in the Process: Mutual Dependence, Distance, and Fragmentation

One important constraint on both donor and recipient is that each is dependent upon actions of the other in order to achieve its own objectives. Although recipients depend on donors for money, this relationship is not one way. For donors depend on recipients both to produce a supply of fundable applications and to implement programs on the local level. The donor does not have the time, the resources, the inclination, and—in many cases—the authority to intervene on a regular basis in the recipient's locality.

Donor and recipient need each other, but neither has the

---

[1] I have found the following to be useful: John D. Montgomery *Foreign Aid in International Politics* (Englewood Cliffs, N. J.: Prentice-Hall, 1967); Montgomery, *The Politics of Foreign Aid: American Experience in Southeast Asia* (New York: Praeger Paperbacks, 1962); Eugene B. Mihaly and Joan M. Nelson, "Political Development and U. S. Economic Assistance" (Paper delivered at American Political Science Association Annual Meeting, New York, 1967); Theodore Geiger and Roger D. Hansen, "The Role of Information in Decision Making on Foreign Aid" in *The Study of Policy Formation*, ed. Raymond A. Bauer and Kenneth J. Gergen (New York: Free Press, 1968); Charles Wolf, Jr., *United States Policy and the Third World* (Boston: Little, Brown, 1967); Robert A. Packenham, "Political Development Doctrines in the American Foreign Aid Program," in *World Politics* 18 (January 1966), pp. 194-235; William Hardy McNeill, *Greece: American Aid in Action* (New York: The Twentieth Century Fund, 1957); C. A. Munkman, *American Aid to Greece: A Report on the First Ten Years* (New York: Praeger, 1958); and Judith Tendler, "Foreign Aid: A Study in Atypical Bureaucracy" and "The Abundance of Foreign Assistance" (Unpublished papers, Department of Economics, University of California at Irvine, 1970).

ability to control fully the actions of the other. Thus, the aid process takes the form of bargaining between partly cooperative, partly antagonistic, and mutually dependent sets of actors.

Because of the geographical space between a donor's home office and the actual project site, bargaining moves must be transmitted over long distances. As we shall see, distance limits the ability of participants to realize certain organizational goals and also contributes to perceptual differences between donors and recipients.

A final constraint on behavior is provided by the institutional fragmentation of both givers and receivers of aid. For donor and recipient do not meet each other as two monolithic forces; rather, each side consists of fragmented groups in which the individual units have differing perspectives and constituencies. This fragmentation, together with competition among the various subunits for funding and authority, is a basic feature of the aid process.

Organizational Objectives

The aid donor typically has the following set of organizational objectives:

1. *Moving Money.*—The donor identifies projects to be funded and then moves the money through its own organization to the recipient. If sufficient money is not being moved, then it may appear to the donor's sponsors (congressmen, for example) that the donor agency is not doing its job.[2]

2. *Information.*—Both before and after project approval, a donor tries to obtain information about the recipient's performance and about the activities of other donor organizations who may be involved in funding related projects.

3. *Control.*—Not only does the donor wish to inform itself about the project; it also attempts to ensure that the project will be carried out in the manner that the donor desires.

4. *Justification.*—The donor takes steps to provide its sponsors with evidence that the projects it funds are worthwhile.

5. *Local Stability and Support.*—The donor seeks stability

in its relations with the recipient, to ensure both a steady flow of fundable projects and a source of information about local events. Beyond this, the donor seeks local allies who will actively support its aims.

The recipient of aid also perceives a set of objectives:

1. *Attracting Money.*—Since a number of other localities and organizations are interested in obtaining outside assistance, a recipient has to take steps to attract the donor's attention—by preparing projects and by preparing literature which extols the virtues of those projects.

2. *Achieving a Steady Flow of Money.*—The recipient wants to have a steady and predictable flow of outside funds so that its own budgeting decisions (including matching fund allocations) can be made with some confidence and so that outside-assisted projects which are started can be continued and completed.

3. *Autonomy.*—The recipient wants to have some independent say about the purposes for which the donor's funds are spent. After all, reasons the recipient, those closest to the local scene are particularly aware of local needs and should have some freedom to shape programs to meet those needs. Another reason for the recipient's desire for autonomy is that it does not want to appear to its own people to be overly dependent on an outside force.

4. *Donor Stability and Support.*—Just as the donor tries to establish stable and supportive relationships in the locality, so the recipient tries to work out a predictable relationship with donor agencies. The recipient hopes that such a relationship will enable it to find out about the donor's intentions as early as possible and to ensure a reasonably steady flow of funds.

These organizational aims and perspectives often lead donors and recipients to prefer different kinds of funding policies. Donors, in their search for control, have a preference for long-term plans, short-term funding, and aid tied to numerous guidelines. Recipients, desiring autonomy and mindful of pressing local needs, are more likely to advocate short-term plans, long-term funding, and aid with few strings attached.

Having sketched out a general model of the aid process, I will now demonstrate how the various elements of that model interact with each other to generate problems for—and conflicts between—donors and recipients. Organizational objectives may be frustrated by structural constraints; the aims of the donor may be opposed to those of the recipient; and the objectives of one participant may be in conflict with each other.

THE DYNAMIC OF THE AID PROCESS: FRAGMENTATION MEETS FRAGMENTATION

Donor and recipient fragmentation appeared in the model as underlying structural features of the aid environment. In both foreign and urban aid experiences, funding agencies have struggled with each other for jurisdiction over programs. An observer of foreign aid has noted that

> The politics of interagency competition is, of course, a well-known phenomenon in Washington. Even among agencies charged with different administrative functions there is enough indirect competition in the search for funds, personnel, and political support to provide distraction from operational routines. But in foreign aid the principal agencies have been in direct competition for funds, for operating and policy responsibility, and even for specific projects. Here the distractions tend to overwhelm the operations.[3]

On the donor side in the United States foreign aid experience, successive aid agencies (such as ICA, AID) and the Departments of State; Defense; Agriculture; Labor; Commerce; and Health, Education, and Welfare have participated in aid programs and have competed for authority.

Urban aid programs have witnessed similar institutional fragmentation and competition. These programs have involved the Departments of Housing and Urban Development; Health, Education, and Welfare; Labor; Commerce; and the Office of Economic Opportunity, among others. As has been the case in foreign aid, component agencies *within* each department often pursue autonomous and contradictory paths. And to complicate matters further, the separate agencies have stimulated their own community coordinating structures—the Com-

[3] Montgomery, *The Politics of Foreign Aid*, p. 153.

munity Action Agencies of OEO, City Demonstration Agencies of HUD, and the Overall Economic Development Program committees of the Economic Development Administration.

The multiplicity of funding organizations finds its counterpart in the existence of numerous independent organizations on the recipient side. Such fragmentation has been noted in developing countries,[4] and it has not been uncommon for other public and private institutions in those countries to compete with the central government in the attraction of outside funds. Dispersed authority has also characterized American urban areas; in Oakland, a report released by a task force of federal officials with responsibilities for programs in that city stated that:

> The fragmentation of authority among the many departments and authorities within the City, and the fact that both welfare and health are the responsiblity of County rather than City departments, make it almost impossible for the City to speak with a unified voice, or to develop across-the-board objectives and priorities which would be acceptable to each autonomous or semi-autonomous section of government. In addition, conflicts over objectives (or the way by which they might be reached) are manifest between citizen groups (the CAA, the Model Cities group) and "the City."[5]

(As we have seen, officials from each level of government are quick to identify what they consider to be excessive fragmentation within other levels.)

Among autonomous "city agencies," disagreement is not a rare occurrence in negotiations surrounding federal programs. In an early model cities meeting, John B. Williams, who as director of the Oakland Redevelopment Agency sat as a city representative on the model cities task force, indicated his agreement on a particular point with the community based West Oakland Planning Committee, rather than the city. His request for a roll call vote of city agencies was turned down by City Manager Keithley. Instances of alliance between the Redevelopment Agency and community groups have been

[4] Albert Waterston, *Development Planning: Lessons of Experience* (Baltimore: Johns Hopkins Press, 1965), pp. 268-269.

[5] Oakland Task Force, San Francisco Federal Executive Board, *An Analysis of Federal Decision-Making and Impact: The Federal Government in Oakland* (San Francisco, 1968; New York: Praeger, 1970), p. 48.

numerous. The mayor may be charged by the charter to carry out intergovernmental relations in the name of the city, but fragmentation of city agencies—buttressed by jurisdictional autonomy, differing views, and differing constituencies—makes it difficult for the mayor to use "the city" as a unified force in dealing with the federal government.

What happens when these two elements of the model—donor fragmentation and recipient fragmentation—meet each other? First of all, the joining of two sets of fragmented units tends to produce a convoluted network of administrative relationships. In Oakland, during 1968, programs in one policy area—manpower—were being funded by five different federal departments, working through five separate state agencies. In addition, numerous county, city-wide, and neighborhood groups and governmental institutions were involved in implementing the programs. Figure 1, showing the institutional relationships involved in those manpower programs, is an impressive illustration of administrative complexity.[6]

Oakland's Cross-Cutting Alliances

The meeting of federal fragmentation and local fragmentation in Oakland has led to the formation of alliances which cut across levels of government. Such a pattern is clearly illustrated by the 1966 dispute over the Neighborhood Centers Pilot Program.[7] This program was launched as the result of a presidential directive to the secretary of HUD, requesting him to establish "in every ghetto in America" a neighborhood center to service the people who live there. HUD, as convening agency, called together four other federal agencies—HEW, OEO, Department of Labor, and Bureau of the Budget—to mount a pilot program in fourteen cities, including Oakland. A joint steering committee, composed of representatives of the agencies involved, was organized in Washington; a similar committee was formed of regional federal officials.

As indications grew that the Oakland Economic Development Council would be designated as the local sponsor of the

[6] Source: Stanford Research Institute, *Human Resources Development for Oakland: Problems and Policies* (Menlo Park, California, 1968).

[7] The following discussion of the neighborhood centers program is based on Oakland Task Force, *An Analysis of Federal Decision-Making and Impact*, pp. 122-129.

neighborhood center program, the HUD regional representative—who was also chairman of the regional steering
committee—sent a letter to HUD in Washington, warning of
the dangers of insisting on OEDC sponsorship. The letter
expressed fears that Mayor Reading might elect to withdraw
the city government from participation in the federal-city task
force experiment which I will discuss later in this chapter. But
the Washington steering committee decided in favor of OEDC
anyway, unless there were "compelling reasons to the contrary." At this point, relations between regional OEO and
regional HUD representatives became strained, with OEO
ranged on the side of the OEDC and HUD appearing to side
with the mayor. Conflict over city sponsorship was paralleled
by a difference of opinion between HUD and OEO staff as
to which federal agency should be convening the program. With
the program's existence at stake, the mayor reluctantly agreed
to accept the federal decision, although he insisted on several
conditions (taken under advisement and later rejected) which
would have limited OEDC's powers. The alliance between the
mayor and regional HUD had been defeated by an alliance
of national HUD, regional OEO, and the OEDC. And institutional fragmentation had facilitated the building of these diverse coalitions.

Difficulties and Opportunities Posed by Fragmentation

Institutional fragmentation complicates the achievement of
organizational objectives for both donor and recipient. Because
of the dispersion of program responsibility among donor agencies, it is often hard for one unit to obtain information on what
another is doing with respect to the same program. And if
authority for a program is shared by a number of funding
agencies, it is harder for each of them to exert control over
the program or to act quickly with respect to it. Oakland's
manpower programs have been the subject of endless negotiation between those diverse federal agencies—Labor, HEW,
EDA, OEO, HUD—who share responsibility for running them.

If fragmentation on the aid-giving side makes it harder for
a donor agency to find out what other donors are doing and
to control the direction of the programs it funds, fragmentation

on the recipient side creates obstacles to a donor strategy of identifying and utilizing local allies to support programs. If recipient officials cannot control other political actors within the locality, then their value to the donor agency is sharply reduced. For recipients themselves, the task of establishing predictable and stable relationships with donors may be complicated by organizational fragmentation and competition among aid-giving units.

Although fragmentation of organizational effort can be a constraint on the achievement of participants' objectives, it need not be looked upon as an unmitigated disaster for those who confront it. Indeed, social scientists have shown that the wide dispersion of organizational authority in the environment of a political leader can provide that leader with flexibility in bargaining. An enterprising political entrepreneur can play other institutions off against each other; he can serve as a mediator between them; or he can avoid unfriendly institutions and build alliances with friendly ones.[8]

The opportunities which fragmentation might offer to recipients have been suggested by organization theorists, who have noted that organizations attempt to increase their autonomy by maintaining a number of alternative sources of support.[9] And students of foreign aid have pointed to the development of alternative aid sources as a possible way to reduce the dependence of recipients upon donors.[10] Thus, we might expect local public officials to find political oppportunities in the dispersion of authority among federal agencies dealing with cities. Not surprisingly, mayors have been among the most vocal critics of proposals to place in each metropolitan area a representative who could speak for the whole federal government.

[8] In *Who Governs?* (New Haven: Yale University Press, 1961), Robert A. Dahl shows how Mayor Lee was able to use a fragmented political environment to pyramid his own influence. And Russell D. Murphy demonstrates that political fragmentation, by providing flexibility and a wide choice of allies, was a crucial ingredient in local administrators' ability to build an innovative poverty program in New Haven. See *Political Entrepreneurs and Urban Poverty: The Formative Years of New Haven's Model Anti-Poverty Project* (Lexington, Mass.: Heath-Lexington Books, 1971).

[9] For example, see James D. Thompson, *Organizations in Action* (New York: McGraw-Hill, 1967), p. 32; and William M. Evan, "The Organization Set: Toward a Theory of Interorganizational Relations," in *Approaches to Organizational Design* ed. James D. Thompson (Pittsburgh: University of Pittsburgh Press, 1966), p. 180.

[10] See Montgomery, *The Politics of Foreign Aid*, pp. 246ff.

With numerous funding channels open, a mayor who is turned down by one departmental unit can appeal to another for help.

From the donor's point of view, fragmentation among recipients can expand the choice of local allies. If one local body will not undertake policies acceptable to the donor, the funding agency can take its business elsewhere—or at least threaten to do so.

An organizationally fragmented environment does not, of course, automatically give a participant the ability to expand political resources. To take advantage of the situation, an actor must have both the taste and capability for political entrepreneurship, for dealing with a complex, fragmented, and often conflictful system. In Oakland, as we have seen, Mayor Reading has tried to bring business standards to politics; he has attempted to simplify the process and make it more rational. Given this outlook, federal fragmentation provides complications, not opportunities. Unlike more politically oriented mayors, Reading has endorsed the appointment of a single federal official who could speak for all departments operating in Oakland.

Because he views contradictory policy preferences among federal departments as inconsistent and inefficient, the mayor has been unwilling to take advantage of fragmentation by allying himself with friendly agencies to oppose unfriendly ones. In the spring of 1969, when the Department of Labor's regional manpower administrator suggested that Reading might convene a county-wide meeting that would set up the local organization for a new federal manpower program, the mayor was reluctant to go forward; he complained that the OEO regional director was probably telling Percy Moore, the anti-Reading director of the local poverty program, that *he* should convene the meeting. Instead of searching for opportunities in federal fragmentation, Reading lost interest in the project. And those federal officials who wanted the mayor to assert himself were disappointed again.

In summary, fragmentation can make it harder for donors to control and find out about programs and for recipients to establish stable and predictable relationships with aid sources. But fragmentation can also offer bargaining opportunities for those with the ability to mediate, negotiate, and play opposing forces off against each other. Such ability is by no means universally held.

Having shown the impact on the aid process of the basic structural condition of fragmentation, let us now consider some further problems of participants and the sources from which they flow.

DONORS' PROBLEMS—AND SOME ATTEMPTED SOLUTIONS

Obstacles to Moving Money

According to the aïd-giving model, the donor's first objective is to move money—to approve projects and then to channel the funds through its own organization and into the hands of the recipient. Moving money is harder than it would at first appear; although recipients' needs usually exceed donors' available supplies, the number of actually financeable projects is often low. For the donor, the constraint of dependence upon a recipient's actions can constitute a critical bottleneck. Recipients may lack sufficient "absorptive capacity," the ability to utilize aid in a productive manner.[11] Furthermore, long delays and considerable staff work for both donor and recipient accompany the assembling and approval of outside assistance proposals. Judith Tendler has written about the problems that this phase of the process has raised for foreign aid officials,[12] and the need to move money rapidly has been a factor in the launching of major urban projects as well. (The EDA job-producing effort in Oakland, discussed briefly in the next chapter, was one project that offered to federal officials the chance to commit funds quickly.)

Distance, Information, and an Unresolved Dilemma

Information about projects, another important need of the donor, is typically hard to get because of the distance between the donor's home office and the site of the project. (Once again, a basic constraint of the system impedes the fulfillment of an organizational goal.) To obtain increased information about

[11] See, for example, Waterston, *Development Planning*, pp. 30ff.
[12] Tendler, "The Abundance of Foreign Assistance," pp. 56-59.

project performance, and to react quickly to recipients' concerns, both foreign and urban aid programs have utilized a system of field or regional officials—donor representatives stationed in the recipient's territory.

In creating a field network, the donor agency exposes itself to a dilemma. Unless the field representatives have the power to make binding decisions on funding commitments, the recipients will express anger and frustration in dealing with them. What is the use, say the recipients, of talking to a donor official unless that official can approve or reject proposals? Mere communication is not enough; it merely raises recipient expectations. These kinds of complaints have been common in both foreign and urban aid programs, leading to demands for decentralization of decision-making authority to field offices.

But there are a number of problems associated with the delegation of increased administrative powers to field offices which should not be overlooked. Agency heads who are held responsible by congress for program performance, and must justify that performance to their sponsors, are reluctant to relax their controls over those programs. And there is always the danger that field officials may become the captives of the interests of the locality or of the strongest political forces within that locality.[13] If a federal urban program is aimed at providing resources to those presently without them, the local capture of a field representative might undermine the program. Thus, a donor may find its organizational objectives in conflict with one another. Allocating more authority to the field might increase the flow of useful information about local conditions, and it can also help to build stable relationships with recipients; but the donor agency's control over programs may be weakened.

Combating Distance and Fragmentation Simultaneously: Foreign and Urban Solutions

In both the foreign and Oakland urban aid experiences, donors have attempted to combat simultaneously the problems posed by the constraints of distance and fragmentation. Foreign

[13] For a discussion of some of the pitfalls of administrative decentralization to field officials, see James W. Fesler, *Area and Administration* (University, Ala.: University of Alabama Press, 1949), pp. 63ff.

and domestic solutions have taken a similar form—the creation of a group of field officials from various aid agencies, who are instructed to cooperate in framing and administering policy. And the reasons for disappointing performances in both cases have also been similar.

Foreign aid's organizational vehicle for this idea was the "country team"; such a team was composed of the ambassador, the chiefs of the aid operations mission, the military advisory group, and the information service, in conjunction with appropriate Washington agencies. But the system did not work as planned; country teams have been found to provide only "general coordination,"[14] with specific aid project decisions made by the technical service divisions of the aid agency. And intradepartmental fragmentation did not lead to more flexibility or a desire to innovate, because each technical division was subject to a strict evaluation from its home office in Washington. New or extraordinary assignments could not be satisfactorily entrusted to regular divisions, because the overall performance of each division was judged by normal technical standards which did not allow for extraordinary functions.[15]

Centralization within each fragmented unit was furthered by the aid agency's personnel system, which "attenuated local control over operations because careers were usually made in Washington, not in the field. A technician's advancement depended more upon assignments made in the technical services in Washington than on any mission director's judgment of his performance in response to local needs."[16] To the extent that aid personnel looked to Washington for guidance, approval, and promotion, the authority of the mission director was weakened. Thus the organization of aid was made up of divided fragments, each of which was under strong central control from Washington. The organizational constructs of "country team" and "aid mission" were there, but career incentives were structured in such a way as to encourage narrow specializations and loyalties.

This organizational experience in foreign aid suggests that, in order to encourage sustained interdepartmental (or even

[14] Montgomery, *The Politics of Foreign Aid*, p. 18.
[15] *Ibid.*, p. 166.
[16] *Ibid.*, p. 167.

intradepartmental) cooperation in the field, there must be some incentive for field staff members to work with representatives of other agencies, and the field staff must have sufficient authority to make such cooperation worthwhile in terms of policy outcomes. Otherwise, collaboration becomes an empty process, having no consequences for action in the world.

In Oakland, from 1966 to 1968, federal officials engaged in a similar attempt at building a cooperative interagency team of field officials. The Federal Executive Board (located in San Francisco) assembled an Oakland Task Force which included regional representatives of federal agencies with program responsibilities in Oakland. Sponsors of the Task Force hoped to produce a common set of priorities for program funding, together with a framework for joint action in the future.

This kind of interagency cooperation, however, proved difficult to effect. In its final report, the Task Force concluded that "there is little consensus among different agencies as to the major problems facing Oakland, or the priority which should be assigned to each." Furthermore, "agency officials tend to define Oakland's problems in terms of their own agency's area of responsibility."[17]

Even if the regional officials had been able to agree on a common list of priorities, cooperation among them would still have been difficult. For there were substantial differences in the amount of authority lodged in various regional offices and, therefore, substantial differences in their ability to commit resources to any cooperative venture. In examining western regional offices relating to Oakland, the Task Force report found that the Small Business Administration was most decentralized, with regional officials able to approve loans. HUD was in an intermediate position, with the region exercising day-to-day responsibility for urban renewal projects, and Washington making decisions about which projects were to be funded. The Departments of Labor, and Health, Education, and Welfare were largely centralized, with most important decisions made in Washington.[18]

A situation in which powers ranged widely from department

[17] Oakland Task Force, *An Analysis of Federal Decision-Making and Impact*, p. 15.

[18] *Ibid.*, p. 101.

to department meant that collaborative agreements would have a tentative nature. Even within departments, there was no guarantee of cooperation at the regional level. In those departments whose units were most strongly tied to Washington, the regional director tended to have little control over that department's component regional parts. Although HUD's regional administrator and SBA's area administrator possessed direct authority over regional organizational components, the regional director of HEW could only be a broker or umpire with respect to his department's various units. Each of the major regional divisions of HEW reported directly to a regional assistant commissioner who in turn reported both to the regional director and to a counterpart commissioner in Washington. Each of the Labor Department's thirteen bureaus and offices operating in the region related "primarily not to each other or a regional coordinator but to their respective counterparts in Washington."[19] Like the foreign aid agencies observed earlier, HEW and Labor may be characterized as systems of centralized fragments.

The organizational lesson of foreign aid's "country team" experience was thus relearned in Oakland. If departments and agencies are run from Washington and if evaluations and promotions are tied to performance within a particular organizational component, then there will be little incentive for interagency collaboration in the field. And even if the field officials are inclined to work out collaborative relationships, their lack of authority raises the question of what result their cooperation could have.

In the Oakland case, there were field offices (HUD and SBA) which had substantial authority to commit funds and which also exercised control over their organization's component parts. But these offices would have found it unsatisfactory to enter into agreements with others who could not commit their agencies to action.

This is not to argue that agencies in Washington should immediately decentralize decision-making authority to the field; we have already seen some of the difficulties inherent in that approach. But it is well to understand that donors

---

[19] Oakland Task Force, *Progress Report I* (San Francisco, 1967), Section 3, p. 3.

cannot triumph over the constraints of distance and fragmentation simply by creating a team of field officials and then urging them to cooperate with each other. For without certain preconditions—an incentive for collaboration and the authority to make it worthwhile—the only certain result of such experiments will be discouragement for the recipient, who expects that such innovative arrangements will bring the aid process closer to the locality. Let us now look more closely at the problems that outside aid poses for the recipient.

THE RECIPIENT'S VIEW: HEADACHES THAT COME WITH AID

To hard-pressed leaders of developing nations or of American cities, outside financial assistance can be a vital aid in the process of successful governance. Physical and social projects can be initiated, political demands can be met, and governments can offer inducements to those groups with whom they wish to ally. But acceptance of outside aid may also bring a host of unforeseen administrative and political difficulties to the recipient.

Unfulfilled Expectations

Based on the experience of United States aid programs in Southeast Asia, Montgomery has written that the "achievements of foreign aid may create new desires faster than the possibilities of meeting them, thus making the inevitable disappointment appear all the greater and more unjust."[20] Desires and expectations can come not only from achievements of aid, but from promises of aid. In Oakland, city officials have complained that federal regional officials raise expectations and then fail to fulfill them. The federal task force in Oakland recorded the following comment from the city manager's office:

If the City people felt that the regional people had real decision-making power, they would have more confidence in going into federal programs. As it is now, there is considerable lack of confidence, based on several experiences. In more than one instance, we've been assured by regional officials that funds would be available, and have submitted applications

[20] Montgomery, *The Politics of Foreign Aid*, p. 18.

on the assurance that they were formalities required before funds could be released. In two cases, our applications were rejected in Washington—once after we had already spent the money.... The Mayor feels that local and regional officials, working together, could develop good programs that would have real relevance to local problems—but the regional people get overruled by Washington.[21]

The problem of unfulfilled local expectations has been a recurring feature of federal urban programs. A study of HUD programs in a number of cities found that the gap between promise and performance had been great in both the turnkey housing and water and sewer grants programs.[22]

Uncertainty and Unevenness of Funding

Frustration and resentment, which may result from expectations that are never fulfilled, can also be caused by expectations that are fulfilled in a slow, uneven, or uncertain manner by the aid donor. According to the model of the aid process, the recipient tries to attract a steady flow of funds—both to inform its own spending calculations and to ensure that projects, once started, will be completed. But in practice, it has been hard for recipient nations or cities to count on the constancy of aid from outside sources.

As Albert O. Hirschman has pointed out: "Since political instability and strenuous competition for pathetically limited public funds are characteristic of many less developed countries, 'external' financial uncertainty has been so prominent an evil that various attempts have been made to 'abolish' it."[23] One attempt at abolition has been the earmarking of special taxes to save favored projects.

The history of foreign aid has produced numerous examples of the perils posed by uncertain funding for the recipient regime. In Greece, for instance, the unevenness and uncertainty of American postwar aid made the position of the Greek government increasingly untenable. Because of Korean War expenditures and Washington's impatience with the slow pace of

[21] Oakland Task Force, *Progress Report III* (San Francisco, 1968), p. 167.
[22] See Dominic Del Guidice, "The City as a Full Partner," *Public Administration Review* 30 (May-June 1970), p. 290.
[23] Albert O. Hirschman, *Development Projects Observed* (Washington, D. C.: The Brookings Institution, 1967), p. 58.

economic and political progress in Greece, American aid to that country dropped from $284.4 million in 1950/51 to $21.3 million in 1953/54.[24] In 1951, the American aid mission began a cutback on all major investment projects in progress by imposing a restriction on the release of counterpart funds. From July 1, 1952, the Greek government was required to finance its own program of capital development from budget surplus over ordinary revenue. The result of American aid cutbacks was painful for the regime, as its opponents fanned public resentment and pointed out how well other recipient countries were doing by comparison.[25] Of course, the recipient government could blame the slowdown on the aid donor—but then it would have to justify its own dependent position.

The donor's action in cutting back aid was not motivated by a desire to incite popular resentment against the local regime, but by the need for funds in other areas and by the donor's judgment that the recipient's programs were not being run in an efficient manner. By regulating the timing of aid, the donor was trying to exercise control over events in the recipient polity. But this attempt at control—a prime organizational objective of the donor—ran into direct conflict with the recipient's goal of maintaining a steady flow of funds.

Although the effect of the aid cutoff was politically painful for the recipient regime, the risks were not all on one side. For considerable resentment was also directed at the United States. When bargaining between donor and recipient results in aid cutbacks, both parties to the bargain may lose. Both donors and recipients have shared interests in the carrying out of programs, as well as conflicting interests as to the ways in which this should be done.

Lack of constancy and certainty in funding has also been present in urban aid programs. Confusion over the availability and level of federal funding for the Neighborhood Centers Pilot Program produced frustration for both poverty program and city officials in Oakland in 1967,[26] and cutbacks in housing, redevelopment, and job-training programs have caused head-

---

[24] See Bickham Sweet-Escott, *Greece: A Political and Economic Survey, 1939-1953* (London: Royal Institute of International Affairs, 1954), pp. 105-106.

[25] See Munkman, *American Aid to Greece* (n. 1 above), p. 281.

[26] Oakland Task Force, *An Analysis of Federal Decision-Making and Impact*, p. 124.

aches for urban aid recipients. In cases in which funding is relatively certain, there may still be opportunities for federal delay. In a discussion of local attitudes toward federal programs, Roscoe C. Martin writes: "There is almost universal criticism of the federal agencies on the ground of delay. Delays of two to three months on handling even routine matters are regarded as normal. A classic example is provided by the efforts of Denver to gain the support of the FAA for a new jet-plane runway. Three long years dragged out between the initiation of this effort and its successful conclusion."[27] When donors' resource constraints, or attempts to influence local policy by cutting back funding, run headlong into recipients' urgent need for money, hostility between participants is inevitable.

Dependence

The recipient in the aid model tries to maintain its autonomy, both in order to exert influence over particular projects and to avoid appearing as a pawn of the donor. Although the aid process is characterized by mutual dependence, the effects of dependence have been particularly severe for recipients. Not only has their autonomy been threatened; some recipients have been thrown out of power because of their acceptance of aid. In the foreign aid experience, a major problem for a recipient regime has been the loss of legitimacy among its own people which can result from perceived dependence on foreign aid. An Indonesian cabinet was forced to resign because it had accepted U.S. aid.[28] And the postwar program of American aid to Greece, a program which is generally considered to have been highly successful, involved the surrender by the Greek government of a large portion of effective sovereignty to the United States.[29] This surrender, which included giving Americans control over the use of foreign exhange and joint control over health policies, provided opposition elements with powerful political ammunition.[30]

The problem of dependence on an outside donor, with the

[27] Roscoe C. Martin, *The Cities and the Federal System* (New York: Atherton Press, 1965), p. 156.
[28] Montgomery, *The Politics of Foreign Aid*, p. 6.
[29] McNeill, *Greece* (n. 1 above), p. 189.
[30] See Sweet-Escott, *Greece*, pp. 105-106.

concomitant development of a power-asymmetrical relationship betwen donor and recipient, has also been present in
federal-city relations in America. For federal funds have not
come to cities without strings attached; the federal donors
supply detailed instructions on the way money is to be used.
Because dependence involves the giving up of some decision-
making authority to the donor (for example, a city's changing
hiring or planning or accounting practices to conform to federal
wishes), there may even be a temptation for a city to opt out
of federal programs. Thus, there is a real tension between the
recipient's objective of attracting funds and its desire for
autonomy.

Guidelines: Donor Control versus Recipient Autonomy

Battles over guidelines or conditions on the use of aid result
from a clash between two features of the aid model: the donor's
desire for control and the recipient's desire for autonomy. To
the recipient, guidelines on spending usually appear as bothersome "strings" imposed by a donor too distant to "understand
the problems of the locality." Ilchman's study of foreign aid
in India showed how numerous conditions placed on the use
of aid tied the hands of the Indian government.[31] And closer
to home, a member of the Oakland city manager's staff complained that

> The strings attached to most federal programs cause all kinds of trouble.
> For instance, there was a big build-up last year on a new jobs program,
> with a lot of publicity which raised a lot of hopes. But there were so
> many restrictions attached that the program couldn't do what we had
> hoped it would. Sometimes there are so many strings that it's hard
> even to spend the money.[32]

Oakland's Building and Housing Department has been
equally critical of administrative guidelines that it views as
restrictive. The Federal Executive Board's task force summarized the department's complaints:

---

[31] Warren F. Ilchman, "A Political Economy of Foreign Aid: the Case of India,"
Asian Survey 7 (October 1967), p. 680.
[32] Quoted in Oakland Task Force, *Progress Report III*, p. 166.

The City is waging a continuing and expensive battle against the spread of blight. However, none of the eleven code enforcement programs now operating in the City is assisted by federal funds, "because the federal code enforcement program has restrictions which make them inappropriate in Oakland." Underground improvements are not an eligible cost, for example, although they are usually required in a federal program.[33]

The complaints of Oakland officials are similar to those noted in other localities. Roscoe Martin found that

> the feeling is widespread among local program executives that the [federal program] manual is applied with too little regard for special situations. One local executive complains of the delay in approving change orders, which frequently leads to increased costs through suspension of work during construction. . . . Still another local executive takes exception to the handling of contracts. Every proposed contract must have the approval of the regional office; this we accept, he says, because the manual requires it. But the regional office keeps each contract between two and three months, and when it comes back to us changes frequently will have been made in minute detail. . . .[34]

Like fragmentation, administrative guidelines can present participants with opportunities as well as problems. Although aid recipients often complain about donors' guidelines, such "strings" can serve as an excuse for a local political leader to put through a new and controversial policy he desires. Schelling has pointed out that, in bargaining, freedom of action is not necessarily an advantage. If a party can arrange to have himself bound to a particular position, then he is unable to concede anything and his bargaining position is therefore strengthened.[35] Because city officials are simultaneously bargaining with federal agencies and with other city actors, they can use federal administrative guidelines to limit their ability to make concessions within the city system. Thus, Mayor Reading was able to use the EDA's insistence on equal employment policies as a powerful argument for initiating an affirmative action minority employment program for the city government—a policy the mayor favored anyway.

Use of this strategy has not, of course, been confined to

---

[33] *Ibid.*
[34] Martin, *The Cities and the Federal System*, pp. 155-156.
[35] See Thomas C. Schelling, *The Strategy of Conflict* (London: Oxford University Press, 1960), pp. 22-28.

Oakland. The study of HUD programs, to which I referred earlier, found that "some city officials are inclined to use the excuse of federal pressures to move in the direction of social reform." These officials appeared to "prefer the prod and protection thus afforded them to self-initiated action which would be contrary to the majority will as they perceive it."[36]

As the aid process unfolds, organizational objectives of the donor are often opposed to those of the recipient. The donor's desire to assert control, for example, may frustrate the recipient's drive for autonomy or the achievement of steady funding. But, as the next section will suggest, donor-recipient differences go deeper than these clashes of institutional goals.

DIFFERENCES IN PERSPECTIVE BETWEEN DONORS AND RECIPIENTS: SUPERMAN AND SHRINKING VIOLET SYNDROMES

Not only do donors and recipients have different and sometimes contradictory sets of specific organizational objectives; they also have fundamentally different perspectives which arise from their different locations and roles with respect to the aid projects themselves. (As we have seen in the last chapter, these perspectives include shared images of their counterparts within the other level of government.) For the donor who formulates broad policy is usually far removed in both distance and spirit from actual project execution, while the recipient is charged with on-the-spot implementation and must live with the local consequences of that implementation. Thus the geographical distance of the model is supplemented by perceptual distance.

Anthony Downs has noted that distance from implementation and its consequences can lead policy makers to fall into a "superman syndrome" of ambitious planning which runs the risk of becoming too broad in scope, of building upon interdependencies which are perceived in theory but which do not exist in the world.[37] Those who are closer to the process of project execution are more likely to exhibit the "shrinking violet syndrome" of limiting their actions to avoid adverse

---

[36] Del Guidice, "The City as a Full Partner," p. 289.

[37] Anthony Downs, *Inside Bureaucracy* (Boston: Little, Brown, 1967), pp. 216-219.

reaction. Thus, federal officials who are removed from immediate contact with—and feedback from—local citizens can afford to advocate sweeping program goals. But local officials, who are often, or perceive themselves to be often, in the line of fire of citizens' complaints, are more inclined to limit their horizons to a range which can be understood and protected. When, as in Oakland, the local officials have an intense dislike of conflict, then the incentives for them to follow "shrinking violet" behavior are further increased. (In chapters 2 and 3, I showed how such behavior has regularly manifested itself in Oakland's City Hall.) Federal-local relations then involve a confrontation between two very different perspectives: superman and shrinking violet. Seen from the federal superman perspective, local caution appears as excessive timidity; seen from the local shrinking violet perspective, federal enthusiasm appears as recklessness. Thus, images are influenced by an actor's place in the aid process.

Relating these two perspectives to the division of authority in the federal system, Martha Derthick has remarked that "separation from local politics and administration gives federal policy makers a license to formulate ideal, innovative objectives, because the political and administrative burdens of the innovations they conceive will be borne locally. They are free, much freer than local officials, to stand publicly for progress and high principle."[38] Derthick notes that when the federal government carries out programs in cooperation with city governments, the problem becomes extreme. Policy makers at the federal level have broad and heterogeneous jurisdictions, and they are separated from administration of actual cases both by numerous layers of organization and by the division of authority between governments in the federal system.[39] When donors formulate policy and recipients are charged with carrying it out, the gap between the two perspectives is large indeed.

It must be noted that the donor's articulation of ambitious goals is related to an important element of the model, the donor's desire to move money. The formulation of exciting and

[38] Martha Derthick, *New Towns In-Town: Why a Federal Program Failed* (Washington, D. C.: Urban Institute, 1972), p. 94.
[39] See *ibid.*, chapter 9, "The Limits of Centralization."

glamorous program objectives is one way to stimulate initial recipient interest and applications.

ATTEMPTS TO BRIDGE THE GAP: CONCENTRATION ON GOALS, RATHER THAN IMPLEMENTATION

As was the case in donor efforts to deal with the problems posed by fragmentation and distance, there have been parallel attempts in foreign and urban aid to bridge the gap between donors and recipients. And, once again, both sets of attempts have run into common difficulties. A basic feature of gap-bridging devices has been the emphasis on building joint commitments to future goals, rather than on devising mutually acceptable procedures to achieve mutually desirable results.

Communication and Priority Setting

One common effort at bridge-building has been the creation of "communications" sessions between the donor's field staff and recipient officials, in order to build agreement around a common list of goals. But such meetings have been frustrating to money-starved recipients, because both country teams in foreign aid and regional representatives in domestic aid have lacked authority to commit funds. Even if goals could be agreed upon, there was no guarantee that any substantive action would follow such agreement.

The forging of agreement around common goals is, in itself, no easy task. In the Oakland Task Force experience, federal-city communications sessions were aimed at drawing up common problem statements and priority lists for donors and recipients. But neither the members of the federal task force nor those of a counterpart task force made up of city officials could agree even among themselves on such priority lists.[40] And as for common statements of Oakland's problems, federal and city representatives failed to agree about the nature of the problems in the crucial areas of health, welfare, and education. For example, federal officials thought that the particularly severe

[40] Oakland Task Force, *An Analysis of Federal Decision-Making and Impact*, pp. 47, 111.

health problems of poor people justified the creation of a special health system to deal with those problems. But the county health department argued that the greatest need was for across-the-board funding to bolster the existing system, which covered all citizens.[41]

Not only were there disagreements over goals and over definitions of the problem; there were more general differences in the objectives and perceptions of the local and federal groups. As the task force report pointed out,

> The federal Task Force was directed to analyze, criticize, evaluate, and recommend; the local Task Force was motivated by a very practical consideration—to get on with action programs, which would bring tangible results. Oakland has had long and intensive experience with the federal presence, and has been "studied to death," as one city official put it. The local Task Force understandably viewed with some doubts another time-consuming study which guaranteed no direct benefits to the city.[42]

The federal task force could not make binding program commitments, and this disappointed city officials. Thus we see the conflict between the donor's desire to devise means for better controlling, evaluating—and thus justifying—its programs, and the recipient's demand for immediate funding. No amount of communication is likely to make this conflict disappear.

Planning

Another device for bringing donors and recipients together in both foreign and urban aid programs has been provided by the introduction of planning mechanisms. Sponsors of such mechanisms reason that, if aid-givers and aid-receivers can join together in charting future events and listing future actions, then differences between them might be reduced.

The trouble has been that plans have often consisted of isolated intellectual exercises, divorced from the difficult decisions involved in budgeting scarce resources. A Bolivian delegate to a Latin-American seminar on planning once remarked: "What is needed is not so much short-term plans as plans

[41] *Ibid.*, pp. 38-39.
[42] *Ibid.*, p. 33.

prepared in a short time."[43] Less developed countries have realized that they have a better chance of attracting foreign financial aid if they are able to produce development plans. Sometimes, in their rush to produce such plans, the technicians have not stopped to consider the preconditions necessary for the implementation of the blueprints. Albert Waterston notes that

> the rapid spread of planning and pressure from aid-giving countries in recent years have ... converted some countries to planning almost solely because it is fashionable and because possession of a national development plan often makes it easier to obtain foreign grants or loans. There are countries where comprehensive plans have been prepared in a few weeks in an office in the capitol without the planners having consulted with operating ministries and agencies.[44]

Brazil's *Plano Trienal* was prepared in this way within ten weeks, and Ghana's Seven-Year Plan (prepared with minimal participation of government operating agencies) took five weeks.[45]

The same process has characterized the formulation of plans which cities must complete to gain federal grants. For example, the EDA requires preparation of an "Overall Economic Development Program," which is supposed to be a comprehensive picture of the local economy—resources, obstacles to economic progress, forward projections of economic health, and so on. But James Sundquist found, on the basis of nationwide interviews, that "OEDPs were prepared because the federal government required them—not because the citizen leaders saw the comprehensive planning process as having enough intrinsic merit to justify the effort."[46] In Oakland, preparation of the OEDP was assigned to a junior member of the Planning Department, an organizational unit which is considerably detached from the day-to-day operation of the city. Preparation of HUD's "workable program" has been similarly viewed by Oakland officials as a bothersome part of the federal application for funds.

---

[43] Quoted in Waterston, *Development Planning*, p. 103.

[44] *Ibid.*, p. 104.

[45] *Ibid.*

[46] James L. Sundquist, with the collaboration of David W. Davis, *Making Federalism Work* (Washington, D. C.: The Brookings Institution, 1969), p. 193.

As has been the case in many developing countries, planners in American cities often tend to view the creation of a plan as an end in itself. With reference to the foreign experience, Waterston writes:

> Where plan formulation is viewed as an exclusive or isolated element divorced in practice if not in theory from plan implementation, as it has in fact been viewed in many countries, one finds that planners pay little attention in their plans to the choice of means to be employed to achieve plan targets. This is why most plans almost always provide detailed information only about *what* is to be achieved, but not about *how* to go about securing development objectives or targets, or about *who* in government or elsewhere should be responsible for carrying out the required tasks.[47]

In 1968, a federally financed study[48] conducted by the Stanford Research Institute urged the city government of Oakland to create a body which would develop comprehensive objectives and strategies in the manpower field, identify programs and funds available from all levels of government, develop a set of priorities, and evaluate all programs in the light of those priorities. Mayor Reading, who was in the midst of trying to gain jurisdiction and funding for City Hall manpower programs, was mystified by these recommendations. What would the city government do after it had carried out all the planning? How would it gain the needed authority and money to implement desired programs? What powers would it have over existing agencies? A Stanford Research Institute representative tried to assuage the mayor's doubts: "When you have a good planning unit, you can easily get control from people." A few months later, Department of Labor regional officials informed the mayor that the real comprehensive manpower planning for the San Francisco Bay Area was being done by CAMPS (Cooperative Area Manpower Planning System), the local "coordinating structure" sponsored by the Department of Labor. After inquiring into the matter, Mayor Reading was surprised to find that the "Oakland representative" on CAMPS had never even been to City Hall.

Instead of viewing planning as an isolated exercise, with

---

[47] Waterston, *Development Planning*, p. 337.
[48] Stanford Research Institute, *Human Resources Development for Oakland*.

implementation either forgotten or thrown in at the end, it would be more useful to consider the planning process as including the totality of governmental choice-making in budgets, in personnel decisions, in daily operation of departments. The separation of planning from implementation, which is encouraged by requirements for "comprehensive" and quickly drawn plans, means that implementation is forgotten and the plan itself becomes the finished product. And comprehensive planning can be worse than irrelevant; it can create problems for a government by making promises to groups which cannot be fulfilled.[49] To be effective, planning must be linked to the operation of government and must provide for implementation. Foreign aid programs have encouraged rapid and overly comprehensive planning by developing countries, and this has resulted in the preparation of plans for their own sake. Urban aid programs, some of which have begun to stimulate a similar process in our cities, can learn something from these disappointing experiences.

Although the preparation of a plan may be used by a recipient as a way to achieve its objective of attracting program funding, the announcement of the plan can create high expectations for a program which might never be fulfilled. By articulating ambitious objectives which are not reached, this kind of planning makes it very unlikely that a related program will be viewed as a success—and the appearance of failure hurts both donor and recipient. Instead of helping aid-givers and aid-receivers identify and capitalize on the areas of agreement between them, overly ambitious planning can make both groups worse off than they were previously.

Although priority setting, communication and planning have been put forward as ways of bridging the gap between donors and recipients, the structures created as vehicles for those strategies have often had the character of pseudo-arenas (see chapter 1), in which real exchanges of resources and commitments to action do not take place. As Schelling would say, they are the sites of *talk*, but not of *moves* which can transmit commitment.[50]

[49] See Sundquist, *Making Fderalism Work*, p. 248.

[50] See Schelling, *The Strategy of Conflict*, p. 117. The distinction between "talk" and "moves" is explained in chapter I of this book.

Even if communication and planning did produce agreement between donors and recipients on general policy goals, many troublesome questions of implementation would remain. The strategies for building agreement discussed here—joint setting of priorities and joint projections of future events—are directed toward goal articulation and policy formulation, but they do not address themselves to the question of how policy is to be implemented. Participants are asked to commit themselves to common goals, but not necessarily to mutually supporting actions. The divorce of policy from implementation is thus exacerbated.

SUMMARY

Going beyond disputes over the proper recipients of federal money, federal and city actors in Oakland have been involved in a recurring pattern of difficult relationships. For these actors are participating in a process of aid-dispensing and receiving, and their behavior is influenced by their organizational needs and problems in that process.

In a general model of the aid process, it is possible to list certain basic features which constrain the behavior of both donors and recipients: mutual dependence among the actors; geographical distance between the aid source and the project; and institutional fragmentation on both donor and recipient sides. In addition, we can posit a number of organizational objectives for those who give or receive aid. The donor's objectives may be seen as (1) moving money; (2) information; (3) control; (4) justification; and (5) local stability and support. For its part, the recipient aims at (1) attracting money; (2) achieving a steady flow of money; (3) autonomy; and (4) donor stability and support.

As the aid process takes shape, the elements of the model interact with each other to produce difficulties for both donors and recipients and to generate conflicts between these groups. There are a variety of ways in which the model's elements may interact. First of all, basic structural constraints can limit the ability of participants to achieve their objectives. Thus, the distance between funding source and project makes it difficult for donors to obtain information about project performance. Second, the objectives of donor and recipient may clash with each other; the battles over administrative guidelines involve a conflict between the donor's insistence on control and the recipient's pursuit of autonomy. Finally, the objectives of one participant may be in opposition to one another. For example, a donor may want a strong field staff for the purpose of attaining better project information and building stable relationships with recipients—but such a staff might build an interest of its own or be captured by the recipient, thus weakening central donor control.

Donors and recipients not only have different sets of organizational objectives; their different locations and roles in the aid process also give them fundamentally differing perspectives with respect to that process. Far removed from the consequences of project implementation, donors tend to be ambitious and far-ranging in the policies they formulate. (Indeed, alluring and dramatic program descriptions can facilitate the stimulation of recipient applications and thus help to achieve an important donor objective—the moving of money.) Recipients, who must live with the immediate reactions to implementation, are often inclined to limit their actions to avoid hostile feedback. Downs characterizes these sharply divergent behavior patterns as the "superman" and "shrinking violet" syndromes.

There have been attempts in both foreign and urban aid programs to bridge the gap between donors and recipients, but the vehicles of these attempts—communications sessions and planning mechanisms—have not been designed to impact on the outside world. And by concentrating on goal articulation and priority setting, these efforts have only furthered the divorce of policy formulation from implementation.

6

Federal Programs, Political Development, and Some Implications for Future Policy

In this final chapter, I will use the Oakland experience in federal-city relations as a base for suggesting some of the ways in which federal programs could be redirected in order to achieve their goals more fully. Although this discussion is directed primarily to the federal actors who have the ability to change the programs, I will also offer some suggestions to local officials. It is important to recognize that the achievement of federal objectives does not exclude or necessarily run counter to the realization of the goals of local political actors. For the game is not zero-sum; donors and recipients do have certain opposing perspectives, but they also have common interests in the completion of substantive programs.

Although this study has focused on Oakland, the kinds of political behavior and policy problems found there are not unique to that city. A perusal of the literature on both foreign and urban aid suggests that there are continuing patterns of behavior in relations between donors and recipients. And the crucial connection between the strength of local leadership and the success of federal programs has been noted in a number of other cities.[1]

[1] See Martha Derthick, *New Towns In-Town* (Washington, D. C.: Urban Institute,

The Oakland Experience

In Oakland, as we have seen, federal programs have had an impact on the distribution of political resources within the city. Certain of those programs—the poverty program, model cities, Neighborhood Development Program, Neighborhood Centers Pilot Program, Concentrated Employment Program—have provided resources for organization to black leaders who are adversaries of the city council. Not surprisingly, the most serious disagreements between federal and local officials in Oakland have centered around federal funding of organizations which are openly hostile to City Hall.

By stimulating mobilization and organization in the black community, federal programs have thus helped to alter the political landscape of the city. But the impact has not been unidirectional; the outcomes of federal programs have themselves been influenced by the characteristics of Oakland's political system. The amorphous, nongroup, nonparty nature of that system has made it difficult to translate poverty organization into effective electoral demands on the city's governmental resources. And political leadership in City Hall, on which federal officials have from time to time counted for program support, has not been forthcoming.

Although federal and local officials argued most vehemently about the selection of local sponsors for certain social change programs, the roots of intergovernmental conflict were found to lie deeper than those specific disagreements. One source of hostility is to be discovered in federal and local officials' images of each other—feds seeing locals as too cautious and narrow, and locals seeing feds as too detached and naive. Another source of conflict lies in the competing organizational objectives of federal donors and local recipients. The donor's desire to assert control, for example, may be in direct conflict with the recipient's drive for autonomy or the achievement of steady funding.

A final problem confronting federal and local officials in Oakland has been the wide dispersion of authority on both levels of government. The federal government and the city face each other as fragmented groups in which individual units have

1972) and Russell D. Murphy, *Political Entrepreneurs and Urban Poverty* (Lexington, Mass.: Heath, Lexington Books, 1971).

differing perspectives. On the federal side, numerous departments and agencies are charged with the responsibility of operating urban programs. And within the city, governmental authority is diffused among a number of autonomous agencies; elected officials in City Hall have been either unwilling or unable to exert control over the actions of these independent bureaucracies. Given this dispersion of power, concerted action on both sides has been difficult to achieve.

With this experience in mind, what advice can we give to policy makers who wish to lessen friction in the system and increase the probability that program goals will be achieved?

SOME INADEQUATE SOLUTIONS

Pseudo-Arenas and Their Costs

Because differences between federal and local representatives go far deeper than misunderstanding and confusion, they are not likely to be resolved by joint boards and task forces which are set up to facilitate communication but which do not have the authority to make program decisions. (The experience of the Oakland FEB Task Force, discussed in Chapter 5, shows the limitations of the "communication" approach.) Nor are intergovernmental relations likely to be improved by requirements for rapid and comprehensive planning exercises, which often have no effect on local decisions regarding budgeting and personnel.

The creation of "pseudo-arenas" is not only unrelated to the processes involved in actually carrying out substantive programs; the building and maintenance of such arenas take valuable time which could be spent elsewhere. And by appearing to promise more than they can deliver, these arenas can contribute to the problem of unfulfilled expectations which is so irritating to those on the local level. Thus, Mayor Reading has been disappointed by regional officials and task forces who have encouraged him to devise programs but who have lacked the jurisdiction to approve and fund them.

In concentrating upon building commitments to goals, rather than on creating a framework for collaborative day-to-day actions, federal decision-makers have tended to separate policy formulation from implementation. And such a separation can pose dangers for a program. A recent book in the Oakland Project series,[2] which traces the tortuous and frustrating path of a federal program in the city, shows how quickly agreement on goals can dissipate into disagreements on the "details" of implementation. The federal Economic Development Administration, the Port of Oakland, and World Airways, Inc. (an Oakland-based airline) reached agreement in 1966 on a program under which the federal agency would supply substantial funds for building public works and the local recipients of those funds would train and hire unemployed blacks. Both federal and local leaders were enthusiastic about this initial agreement, but the program bogged down during the following months and years over questions of financing, bay fill, construction, and the competing jurisdictions of diverse agencies and offices.

Besides demonstrating the tenuous nature of agreement on initial goals, the experience of this program shows how the dispersion of governmental authority in the American political system provides numerous groups with the power to block programs. A diverse group of federal and local agencies became involved when they felt their interests being impinged upon, and their actions often caused program delay.

Finally, the EDA effort in Oakland is a good example of a federal program that was hurt by the lack of local leadership. Federal officials had counted on Mayor Reading, who supported the program, to help them make it a success. But they were to discover that the mayor had neither the resources nor the inclination to enforce his will on other local political actors.

Federal policy makers had devoted great effort to securing an initial program commitment, but they underestimated the difficulties which both the federal and local systems posed for implementation. If we are to suggest improvements in federal urban programs, we must look to means other than collaborative goal-setting.

[2] Jeffrey L. Pressman and Aaron B. Wildavsky, *Implementation* (Berkeley and Los Angeles: University of California Press, 1973).

Revenue Sharing

Revenue sharing—the provision of money by the federal government to cities, with few or no strings attached—might appear to deal with some of the basic sources of friction and discontent in federal-city relations. Under this program, local officials are relieved of some of the restrictive administrative guidelines they so often denounce. Furthermore, the power asymmetry and irritation produced by constant local dependence on federal officials' decisions might be expected to be eased. With an infusion of relatively unencumbered financial resources, city officials should have less need to beg.

But there are serious political problems connected with revenue sharing. One is that, although revenue sharing may reduce the power asymmetry between federal and city governments, it may *increase* the resource imbalance among groups within the city. If a goal of federal urban policy is to redistribute resources in cities to people and neighborhoods who presently lack them, categorical grants can have the advantage of earmarking funds for use in certain poorer areas. (For example, the Elementary and Secondary Education Act's Title I program for compensatory education provides funds only for schools that meet certain poverty criteria.) Unrestricted revenue sharing might be divided up by powerful interests in a community, with weaker political actors getting short shrift.

Furthermore, merely increasing the flow of revenue to cities does not deal with the quality of political leadership and political institutions at the local level, factors which can have an effect on the implementation of federal programs. Formulae for distributing funds largely on the basis of population offer no incentives for local governments to expand the scope and effectiveness of their programs. And even those revenue sharing proposals that attempt to reward local government capacity[3] end up defining that primarily in terms of planning capability or administrative efficiency.

[3] Such as the proposal put forth by Senator Humphrey and Representative Reuss in 1971. (See "White House Set to Compromise on Fund Sharing," *The New York Times*, Feb. 23, 1971, p. 1.)

In his State of the Union Address in January 1971, President Nixon declared that revenue sharing would have a dramatic effect on local governments: "If we put more power in more places, we can make government more creative in more places. For that way we multiply the number of people with the ability to make things happen—and we can open the way to a new burst of creative energy throughout America."[4] In fact, it is not at all clear that increased financial resources can by themselves create strong and responsive government at the local level. We have already seen that there is considerable variability in local leaders' use of outside resources. If local governmental leaders have made a practice of avoiding conflict and underutilizing their own resources, why should the new revenue make them suddenly adventurous? It is more likely that such leaders will use the money either for local tax relief or for meeting the increasingly aggressive demands of city employees' unions.

We have observed that federal programs can be vitiated by the absence of strong political bodies at the local level, and by the lack of effective arenas where federal and local officials can bargain over political resources. Neither planning, communicating, nor revenue sharing are adequate to deal with what are essentially political problems: the creation of viable sites for the exchange of resources and the mobilization of public support for programs. Therefore, it seems reasonable to suggest that policy makers should be concerned with increasing the capacities of political systems themselves—both federal and local. Social scientists have dealt with these issues in the study of political development. But "political development" has been discussed by these scholars in a number of different ways, and we must be more specific in our analysis and our advice.

AID STRATEGY AND POLITICAL DEVELOPMENT

Definition and Alternative Approaches

Although many meanings of political development have been suggested, students of the subject usually include two elements

[4] President Nixon's State of the Union Address, January 22, 1971.

in their definitions: (1) the ability of a wide range of people to participate in politics and make demands on government, and (2) the ability of government to satisfy those demands.[5] I will define political development as "the capacity of a political system both to articulate people's needs and to respond to them effectively." There must be a balance between the demand for political resources and the supply of them, but this balance cannot be achieved by the choking off of effective demand.

Scholars have differed on the conditions which they identify as the prime correlates or determinants of political development.[6] One common view is the *economic* approach, which treats political development as primarily a function of a level of economic development sufficient to serve the material needs of the people and to enhance a reasonable harmony between aspirations and satisfactions.[7] If a man's material needs are satisfied, argue the adherents of this approach, he can spend the time needed to participate in politics—and he may have financial resources with which to participate. On the supply side of the political development definition, economic development can provide a government with the wherewithal to meet increased demands.

Another group of writers has taken the *administrative* approach, arguing that political development is primarily a function of the administrative capacity to maintain law and order efficiently and to perform governmental output functions rationally and neutrally.[8] The case for political development in terms of advanced administration was argued persuasively by Max Weber.[9]

[5] See, for example, Lucian W. Pye, "The Meaning of Political Development," *The Annals of the American Academy of Political and Social Science* 358 (March, 1965), pp. 4-13; Gabriel A. Almond, "A Developmental Approach to Political Systems," *World Politics* 17 (January 1965), pp. 183-214; Warren F. Ilchman and Norman Thomas Uphoff, *The Political Economy of Change* (Berkeley and Los Angeles: University of California Press, 1969), p. 48.

[6] For a helpful summary of diverse views on the subject, see Robert A. Packenham, "Approaches to the Study of Political Development," *World Politics* 17 (October 1964), pp. 108-120.

[7] See *ibid.*, pp. 110-113. See also Seymour Martin Lipset, *Political Man* (Garden City, N. Y.: Doubleday, 1959), chapter 2. Lipset links economic development to democracy.

[8] See Packenham, "Approaches to the Study of Political Development," pp. 113-115.

[9] See chapter 8, "Bureaucracy," in *From Max Weber*, ed. H. H. Gerth and C. Wright Mills, (New York: Oxford University Press, 1946).

Still another approach is provided by those who stress widespread social *mobilization* or *participation* in public affairs as the primary facilitator of political development.[10] Karl Deutsch has stated that modernization—increases in literacy, urbanization, exposure to mass media,—has expanded the "politically relevant strata of the population," has multiplied the demands for government services, and has thus stimulated increased governmental capabilities.[11]

Having seen some of the ways in which social scientists have treated political development, we must now ask whether aid donors are concerned with the effects of their assistance on the political development of the recipient. Do donors pay attention to politics? What approaches, if any, do they take to the subject of political development?

Aid Donors and Political Development

After interviewing fifty-four foreign aid officials, Robert A. Packenham concluded: "Our examination shows that while the declared purpose of American foreign aid is to help create 'a community of free nations cooperating on matters of mutual concern, basing their political systems on consent and progressing in economic welfare and social justice,' the doctrines of AID and aid administrators in other agencies indicate little explicit attention to political development."[12] The author found that the approach to political development relied upon most often was the economic one, and even then it was only implicit.[13] In a memorable quotation, a chief planning officer in one of the aid regions told Packenham: "You know, one thing I've never been clear about is what our fundamental policy is on the question of whether we're trying to promote democracies or not."[14]

Although many federal donors of urban aid tend to view their assistance as financially beneficial and politically neutral, my interviews with federal officials and my observations of their

[10] See Packenham, "Approaches to the Study of Political Development," pp. 115-117.
[11] Karl W. Deutsch, "Social Mobilization and Political Development," *American Political Science Review* 55 (September 1961), pp. 493-514.
[12] Packenham, "Political Development Doctrines in the American Foreign Aid Program," *World Politics* 18 (January 1966), p. 229.
[13] *Ibid.*, p. 211.
[14] *Ibid.*, pp. 211-213.

activities in Oakland did uncover some examples of donors' concern with development of the recipient polity. They were not merely technical people, ignoring politics. Some EDA officials espoused the economic approach to political development; if minorities had jobs and money, these officials asserted, they could begin to play a larger role in the city's political system. (EDA people tended to combine this economic approach with an endorsement of group pluralism. If the blacks, the mayor, and the Port were all given some resources, then they would come together to talk about specific programs, instead of fighting each other with empty slogans.)

Other federal officials in Oakland followed the administrative approach to political development. Department of Labor representatives persisted in encouraging the mayor to develop an efficient manpower planing unit, on the grounds that increased political authority would eventually flow to those with demonstrated administrative capacity. And a third group of donors favored the participation approach; OEO representatives and HUD sponsors of model cities talked about the crucial need to mobilize poor people to press their demands in the public arena.

The Importance of Political Institutions: Local and Federal

Although certain federal officials have given attention to the political effects of their programs, it is not clear that the economic, administrative, and participatory approaches are sufficient to go to the heart of the problem. In Oakland, even if people in the city received more money, the lack of effective groups and parties would make it difficult for the citizens to use their new financial resources in the political arena. Even if the city government's administration were made more efficient, local political leaders would not automatically move to expand the city's jurisdiction and increase its responsiveness to diverse citizen demands. And even if more poverty groups were mobilized, the amorphous nature of Oakland politics would make the transition from the federal program arena to the city's electoral arena a difficult one.

Thus, *the weakness of political institutions and the absence of political leadership* have combined to limit both citizens'

effective demands on government and government's willingness
and ability to respond. The virtual non-existence of political
groups and parties has deprived leaders of support for programs
and information about citizens' preferences, and the elected
leaders themselves have shown a marked tendency to avoid
conflict and to contract their job jurisdiction rather than
expand it. This pattern of local political behavior has meant
that federal officials have lacked effective partners on the local
level who could help them implement programs.

One desirable policy aim, therefore, might be the strengthening of local political institutions. This side of political development has been less thoroughly treated by social scientists. As
Packenham has written, "More than anything else in recent
years, political development has meant participation and social
mobilization. The need to harness, control, organize, and put
to work this process of social mobilization has been less well
perceived than has the need to get it started."[15] One student
of political development who has defined the process in terms
of harnessing, channeling, and organizing political action is
Samuel P. Huntington,[16] who defines political development as
"the institutionalization of political organizations and procedures."[17] Institutionalization is "the process by which organizations and procedures acquire value and stability."[18] Thus, for
Huntington, political development takes place as societies learn
"the art of associating together,"a phrase he takes from De
Tocqueville.[19] Without strong political institutions, says the
author, society lacks the means of defining and acting upon
its common interests. Huntington's treatment of political development as the strengthening of political institutions seems
well directed to the Oakland experience, in which the weakness
of such institutions has been a prime reason for citizens'
inability to press effective demands and the political system's
inability to respond.

A particularly important institutional weakness in Oakland
has been that of the city government, which has lacked both

[15] *Ibid.*, p. 202.
[16] Samuel P. Huntington, "Political Development and Political Decay," *World
Politics* 17 (April 1965), pp. 386-430.
[17] *Ibid.*, p. 393.
[18] *Ibid.*, p. 394.
[19] See *ibid.*, p. 386.

the jurisdiction and the will to take action in the policy areas of redevelopment, housing, education, manpower, and poverty programs. Ilchman and Uphoff have noted the existence of a "vicious circle of weak authority" in developing countries: Governments lack control over other institutions and resources; the demand for participation in government is therefore low; and given a low demand for governmental resources, the government has trouble in getting its way with other actors. The authors conclude: "One thing is clear. The more skillfully the statesman uses the authority he has, the greater [nongovernmental actors'] demand will be for influence and a share in authority."[20] Thus, it can be argued that more aggressive action on the part of government will result in more demands being made in the governmental arena—intensified attempts to win electoral office and to influence the behavior of elected officials. Because competitive electoral activity can provide a way for citizens to influence the allocation of public resources, and also offer incentives for public actors to build constituencies and join in framing common programs, it is worth searching for policies that make electoral activity more likely. If federal policies can help to increase the worth and the scope of local government, this might encourage electoral attempts to take over the government. (It might be argued that revenue sharing, by increasing the resources available to local governments, could make those governments more desirable targets for electoral activity. In this way, revenue sharing might make a contribution to local political development. But the problems with this approach, which were discussed earlier, remain serious.)

An increase in the power of local government does not, of course, equal political development in the local system. After all, definitions of political development have usually included the capacity of a political system to articulate and respond to a wide range of citizen demands. And a continuing concern of federal urban policy makers has been that the responsiveness of local government to the demands of citizens—particularly poor people and minorities — should be increased. Thus, federal policy might well be directed in ways that would encourage

[20] Ilchman and Uphoff, *The Political Economy of Change*, p. 86.

local governments to be both stronger and more open.

Strengthening elected officials and making local government more responsive to the needs of poor people are not mutually exclusive policies. As Duane Lockard has stated, the dispersal of local power to non-elected bureaucracies has made it extremely difficult for poor and black people to influence policy outcomes. He has remarked that

> the dispersal of power to the housing bureaucracy, urban renewal authorities, the police department, and welfare agencies have done much to bring to climax the conditions of the large city. If black people are the victims of these scattered powerful bodies, and they assuredly are in city after city, and there is little means to assert control over these agencies (also true), then it follows that one factor making for the explosiveness of the present situation is dispersal of power.[21]

The development of strong and open local institutions would make a city's political system better able to articulate and respond to its citizens' demands, as well as providing potential sources of support for federal programs. If federal policy is to be concerned with local political development, then it must go beyond economic, administrative, and participatory approaches to build and strengthen political institutions themselves.

Thus far, the discussion has focused on political weakness and development on the local level. But it would be inaccurate for federal officials to assume that local inadequacies constituted the only obstacles to the successful completion of federal programs. Indeed, we have seen that the federal aid system itself is characterized by a lack of effective arenas in which the exchange of political resources can take place. Just as there is a need at the local level to develop the capacity to respond to citizens' needs, there is a need in the federal system for institutions and processes that will respond to the concerns of local officials.

Once again, it is important to recognize that the federal-city relationship is one of mutual dependence. And if federal officials can pursue policies which will influence the development of local government, so local officials can act to increase the

[21] Duane Lockard, "Value, Theory, and Research in State and Local Politics" (Paper delivered at the annual meeting of the American Political Science Association, 1970), p. 9.

responsiveness of the federal government. Recognizing federal fragmentation and diversity, they can play federal agencies off against each other to gain more for themselves. Furthermore, local officials from different cities can join together (as a number of big-city mayors have done) to demand increased resources from the federal government. By asking that federal performances more closely match promises, local officials can help to change pseudo-arenas into effective arenas within the federal system.

Toward Future Policy

Federal and Local Assessments

Because a local political system can have a strong effect on the outcomes of federal programs, it behooves federal officials to assess early the capability of local political leaders and institutions. If local political officials lack the power to influence other institutions and people, then they will be of little value as "partners" in federal programs.

The strength of local institutions varies from city to city, and federal policy ought to take that into account. For example, during the 1960s the federal Economic Development Administration expected local officials in both Chicago and Oakland to "lean on" local recipients of EDA funds in order to convince them to hire unemployed minorities. In Chicago, strong mayoral leadership produced compliance on the part of the recipient; in Oakland, there was no political leader or group who could produce the same result.

Federal agencies ought not to assume that all local governments and leaders are potentially helpful vehicles for their purposes. In cities where such is not the case, measures—such as those I will discuss shortly—might be taken to increase institutional capacity.

For their part, local officials should try to assess the likelihood of a given federal program's actual arrival and completion. Before entering into planning exercises and telling local citizens about potential federal funding, city leaders should try to get commitments both on money and on federal assistance in the implementation stage. The cycle of bright promises, raised expectations, and ultimate disappointment has been repeated too often.

It is important to remember, however, that these kinds of assessments are not costless for the individuals and organizations involved. As was pointed out in chapter 4, efforts by federal and local officials to find out about each other are fraught with difficulty, and expensive in terms of the time and effort involved. In suggesting possible changes in officials' behavior, we must be careful to look at the costs involved in making those changes.

Building Institutions

There are a number of ways in which future policy could be designed to increase the strength and responsiveness of both local governments and the federal system itself. First, the federal government could help city governments to increase their financial resources by providing increased credits toward federal income tax for the local taxes a citizen had paid. This would not be a policy of providing funds to cities on the basis of population criteria, with the hope that the money would then stimulate local government to increase the scope of its activities. Rather, the tax-credit system would provide incentives for local governments to raise their own revenue. Local revenue increases would then be tied to local effort, with the federal government providing an assist.

Second, federal agencies could tie funding to local actions which would expand the authority, capacity, and openness of local government. During 1970 and 1971, for example, the HUD area office with responsibility for Oakland took a number of steps designed to encourage the city government to expand its authority and increase effective citizen prticipation. Funds for HUD projects were held up in late 1970 because a broadly based citizens' committee was not judged to be participating enough in redevelopment decisions.[22] Furthermore, the HUD area director strongly urged the Oakland City Council to involve itself more deeply in the redevelopment process by requiring the council to review in detail and then pass upon

[22] "OCCUR Approved by Council," *Oakland Tribune*, October 30, 1970.

Redevelopment Agency projects. And HUD returned plans for the City Center project, on the grounds that city government leaders had not had adequate opportunity to examine them first. (It is no coincidence that the HUD area director who made these decisions was James H. Price, formerly administrative assistant to Mayor Reading. Price had observed the performance of Oakland's elected officials at close range.)

Another HUD attempt to expand city government's authority came in 1971, when Area Director Price held up $3 million in housing funds, citing the Oakland Housing Authority's administrative difficulties and its failure to provide social service programs for tenants. The HUD official urged the city council to take on more authority in the housing field, and offered federal assistance for City Hall efforts to exercise greater control over the housing authority.[23] Thus, a federal agency was directly encouraging Oakland's elected leaders to abandon their habit of conflict avoidance and to act in a more aggressive and more public manner.

Besides making city government stronger, federal policy can also be directed toward making that government more open to the policy demands of a wide range of citizens—especially the poor, who are most in need of public social services. We have seen the difficulty of moving from participation in Oakland's poverty program arena to making an effective demand on the city's governmental resources. Rather than merely encouraging participation for its own sake, federal policy ought to devise ways of ensuring that participation will mean something in terms of ongoing programs and the allocation of resources. Policies can be designed that will encourage the building of links between poverty organizations and the city government. For example, in Oakland's model cities program, neighborhood representatives and city officials each have a veto over program decisions. Before a project is approved, both groups must signify their assent. This "double green light" approach means that participation can have a real effect on programs.

Third, local and federal officials can enter into longer-range agreements which can both strengthen local elected officials and create effective sites for bargaining in the federal process.

[23] "U. S. Prods Council on Housing," *Oakland Tribune*, June 18, 1971.

In late 1970, the HUD regional office in Chicago entered into a negotiated agreement with the city of Gary, Indiana. Under the terms of the agreement, HUD pledged to fund a list of projects desired by the city. In return, the city committed itself to achieve federally set objectives in a number of areas: equal opportunity employment; building of low-cost housing; modernization of codes; and improvement of city capacity. HUD made a particular effort to bolster the position of the city government and of the mayor. Formerly, HUD pograms had had their own diverse client agencies. But under this arrangement, the city government was treated as the client and the mayor was designated as its spokesman. On the HUD side, one person represented the HUD regional administrator and had decision-making power for all agency program areas.[24]

This kind of arrangement is tailored to avoid the constant battling over guidelines which so often irritates both donors and recipients. Unlike unrestricted revenue sharing, it does tie federal funding to specific city efforts in certain fields, but the standards are set as the result of federal-city negotiation. In this situation, discussions between federal and city representatives are not merely attempts at fostering communication and understanding; the negotiations result in real commitments on programs and resources. Furthermore, federal cooperation is not limited to the goal-setting stage; the federal agency pledges itself to help the city on a continuing basis in the process of implementation. Thus, the gulf between policy formulation and implementation may begin to be closed. And the prospect of future annual negotiations provides an incentive for both sides to live up to the agreements they made.

With the advantage of such a system in mind, HUD decided to replicate the Gary model in its dealings with a number of other cities. By March 1973, the federal agency had negotiated "annual arrangements" with seventy-nine cities.[25] Oakland was one of those cities; after a series of meetings, federal and local officials there agreed on mutually acceptable terms in February 1972.[26] According to the arrangement, HUD committed itself

---

[24] See "The Gary Arrangement," *Model Cities Service Center Bulletin* 2 (February-March, 1971), pp. 4-6.
[25] See *National Journal* 5 (March 3, 1973), pp. 301ff.
[26] *Memorandum of Agreement Between The City of Oakland, California, and the*

to fund a wide range of specific renewal, housing, open space, and water and sewer projects. For its part, the city government agreed to undertake a number of actions desired by the federal government—strengthening of affirmative action hiring and contracting policies, increasing city efforts in relocation, developing increased administrative capacity in City Hall, and so forth. Instead of stopping at the goal-setting stage, federal and local officials continued to meet as various parts of the agreement were being put into effect.

Oakland's early experience with the annual arrangement[27] illustrates both strengths and potential pitfalls in the program. City officials were enthusiastic about the greater degree of certainty provided in the project-funding process. Both federal and City Hall representatives noted with approval the reduction in fragmentation produced by a consideration of diverse projects at one time. There was agreement that city government actors had become more involved with decisions regarding redevelopment and housing programs. And it was also suggested that centralizing decision-making on projects made it easier for citizens' groups to concentrate their efforts at persuasion.

But the annual arrangement did have its problems. Because of uncertainty over its own funding for the coming fiscal year, HUD could not give ironclad commitments on the funding levels for approved projects. City officials continued to resent what they perceived as federal dominance in intergovernmental meetings, and federal and local officials' images of each other continued to provide a source of hostility between the officials. Thus, federal insistence on local actions regarding minority hiring or open housing were regarded by locals as further examples of federal naiveté, while local resistance to these ideas was regarded by the feds as another example of the locals' narrowness and excessive caution. (As we have seen in chapter 4, steps taken by each side to deal with the felt shortcomings of the other can have the effect of strengthening unfavorable images on both sides.)

Further problems were caused by recurring bureaucratic

U. S. Department of Housing and Urban Development. Approved by the City Council, February 10, 1972.

[27] As related in extended interviews with both federal and local officials during the summer of 1972.

rivalries among local officials. The Planning Commission and the Redevelopment Agency were each attempting to gain control over the city's relocation effort, and various agencies— most notably Redevelopment—were accused by City Hall people of trying to "make end runs" around the annual arrangement and negotiate directly with federal officials. Finally, city councilmen and administrators once again manifested a "retrenchment syndrome" in their cautious approach to acquiring new power. They recognized that increased authority over HUD programs would mean increased headaches for them. As one councilman put it: "Of course, this puts the city on the spot. Everybody can come to the city and complain—'why didn't we get more?' The old way, they'd complain to outside agencies." With their marked distaste for conflict Oakland city officials did not look upon the annual arrangement as an unmixed blessing.

Thus, it should not be expected that annual arrangements can summarily abolish deep-seated obstacles to concerted action within the federal and local political systems. But this program is worth mentioning as a way in which federal policy can be designed to provide increased opportunities for local elected officials and to build a continuing framework for collaboration between federal and local actors.

Payment for Performance. . . .

Directness is a useful criterion to keep in mind in creating program incentive systems. If federal donors desire to simulate the development of strong and responsive political institutions at the local level, they ought not merely to share revenue with cities and then hope that the additional money will make city governments more responsive to citizens' needs. Rather, they should explore ways of rewarding cities for specific achievements: raising local taxes to finance expanded services; instituting an equal employment policy for city jobs; or building a required number of low-cost housing units. Revenue sharing should be based on a formula which rewards those city governments that are making a concrete effort to increase their capability and expand their services.

. . . Not for Planning

Too often, federal programs require local planning rather than evidence of local performance. EDA has required preparation of an Overall Economic Development Program before funds can be received; HUD has insisted upon preparation of a "workable program." Cities have been careful to produce the required plans, but there is no guarantee that the plans will be related to decisions involving the allocation of city resources.

Instead of treating planning as an isolated exercise, with implementation either forgotten or thrown into the end, it would be more useful to consider the planning process as including the totality of governmental decisions: in budgets, in personnel choices, in the daily operation of departments. The separation of planning from implementation, which is encouraged by requirements for "comprehensive" and quickly drawn plans, means that implementation is forgotten and the plan itself becomes the finished product. To be effective, planning must provide for implementation. If federal rewards are tied to performance, then local officials have an incentive to carry out such plans that will help them improve performance; the distinction between planning and implementation is broken down. Federal assistance ought not to be given simply to help cities improve their "planning capacity"; rather, money should be made available for hiring staff assistants who can help city officials actually carry out projects. (In order to influence federal action, local officials might jointly demand that federal planning funds be made available for needed staff work and be related to projects that will actually materialize.)

Using the System: Benefits in Apparent Adversities

In recommending changes in federal urban programs, we should keep in mind not only the costs of the change suggested, but also the likelihood of that change being adopted. Certain enduring features of the federal system have proved, and will continue to prove, resistant to various reformers' attempts to wish them away: the broad dispersion of power among different levels of government and different agencies at the same level; bureaucratic rivalry and imperialism; the tendency of those who give away money—at whatever level of government—to put certain conditions on its use; and sharp differences of opinion among political actors as to what public priorities should be.

It would be a mistake, however, to regard all of the causes of difficulty and tension in the federal system as insurmountable obstacles to the exercise of political leadership or the achievement of desirable social objectives. Indeed, what appear as problems in the system may serve certain advantageous purposes. For example, federal guidelines—the "strings" so often condemned in local officials' oratory—can provide excuses for local officials to enter into redistributive social programs that they would judge impossible to initiate otherwise. Pleading that they are constrained by federal strings, local officials can actually enlarge their freedom of action.

Or, take the case of fragmentation. Although the dispersion of governmental authority obviously poses serious problems for the successful implementation of programs, it also provides political actors with multiple access points within the political system. If one agency is not receptive to their requests, then another might be tried. Or agencies may be played off against one another. (Of course, the ability to utilize fragmentation in this way requires certain skills of political entrepreneurship—which, as we have seen, are not universally held.)

Thus, keeping in mind the likely persistence of certain features of the federal aid system, we can both suggest desirable changes in that system and also point out some of the ways in which apparent sources of difficulty can be seen as political opportunities.

SUMMARY

Because disagreements between federal donors and local recipients involve more than confusion and misunderstanding, such differences are not likely to be ended by joint committees created to facilitate "communication." Revenue sharing, which would appear to deal with one cause of intergovernmental friction by reducing the resource imbalance between federal and local governments, may increase other resource imbalances between have and have-not groups within the city.

Furthermore, it is far from evident that the mere infusion of financial resources would cause city governments to expand the scope of their activities and attempt to meet more citizen demands. We have seen that an amorphous, nongroup local political system, featuring a retrenchment-oriented city government, can deprive federal officials of a local force needed to aid program implementation. And we have also seen that the federal system itself lacks effective arenas in which donor-recipient bargaining over political resources can take place. Therefore, it seems reasonable to urge that future programs should concern themselves with both local and federal political development. But political development—defined here as "the capacity of a political system both to articulate people's needs and to respond to them effectively"—has been treated in different ways by social scientists. Some students of the subject have followed an economic approach, while others have focused on administrative or participatory paths to political development. And a number of federal officials have followed one or another of these approaches in defining the goals of their programs.

But more money, increased administrative efficiency, and heightened levels of participation may not by themselves lead local governments or intergovernmental systems to be stronger and more open. Therefore, federal policy ought to be framed with the specific intention of increasing the capacity and responsiveness of political institutions themselves. And this might be done in ways that reduce the need for constant planning exercises and administrative haggling between levels of government, which are present sources of discontent among both donors and recipients. By building the framework for commitments to continuing joint action, instead of frustrating goal-setting, both federal and local officials can gain.

Bibliography

1. *Books*

Almond, Gabriel and Sidney Verba. *The Civic Culture*. Boston: Little, Brown, 1965.

Banfield, Edward C. *Political Influence*. New York: The Free Press, 1961.

Bradford, Amory. *Oakland's Not For Burning*. New York: David McKay Co., 1968.

Dahl, Robert A. *Who Governs?* New Haven: Yale University Press, 1961.

Derthick, Martha. *New Towns In-Town*. Washington, D.C.: Urban Institute, 1972.

Downs, Anthony. *Inside Bureaucracy*. Boston: Little, Brown, 1967.

Elazar, Daniel. *American Federalism: A View from the States*. New York: Thomas J. Crowell Company, 1966.

Fesler, James W. *Area and Administration*. University, Ala.: University of Alabama Press, 1949.

Gerth, H. H. and C. Wright Mills, *From Max Weber*. New York: Oxford University Press, 1946.

Graves, W. Brook. *American Intergovernmental Relations*. New York: Charles Scribner's Sons, 1964.

Hirschman, Albert O. *Development Projects Observed*. Washington, D.C.: The Brookings Institution, 1967.

Ilchman, Warren F. and Norman Thomas Uphoff. *The Political Economy of Change*. Berkeley and Los Angeles: University of California Press, 1969.

Jervis, Robert. *The Logic of Images in International Relations*. Princeton: Princeton University Press, 1970.

Kramer, Ralph M. *Participation of the Poor*. Englewood Cliffs, N.J.: Prentice-Hall, 1969.

Lawrence, Paul R. and Jay W. Lorsch. *Organization and Environment*. Boston: Harvard Business School, 1967.

Leach, Richard H. *American Federalism.* NewYork: W. W. Norton, 1970.
Lipset, Seymour Martin. *Political Man.* Garden City, N.Y.: Doubleday, 1959.
Lubell, Samuel. *The Hidden Crisis in American Politics.* New York: W. W. Norton, 1970.
Martin, Roscoe C. *The Cities and the Federal System.* New York: Atherton Press, 1965.
McFarland, Andrew S. *Power and Leadership in Pluralist Systems.* Stanford, Calif.: Stanford University Press, 1969.
McNeill, William Hardy. *Greece: American Aid in Action.* New York: The Twentieth Century Fund, 1957.
Meier, Gerald M. *International Trade and Development.* New York: Harper and Row, 1963.
Montgomery, John D. *Foreign Aid in International Politics.* Englewod Cliffs, N.J.: Prentice-Hall, 1967.
———. *The Politics of Foreign Aid: American Experience in Southeast Asia.* New York: Praeger Paperbacks, 1962.
The Municipal Year Book. Washington: International City Managers' Association, 1968.
Murphy, Russell D. *Political Entrepreneurs and Urban Poverty: The Formative Years of New Haven's Model Anti-Poverty Project.* Lexington, Mass.: Heath, Lexington Books, 1971.
Neustadt, Richard. *Presidential Power.* New York: John Wiley, 1960.
Polsby, Nelson W. and Aaron B. Wildavsky. *Presidential Elections.* New York: Charles Scribner's Sons, 1968.
Report of the National Advisory Commission on Civil Disorders. New York: Bantam, 1968.
Schelling, Thomas C. *The Strategy of Conflict.* New York: Oxford University Press, 1960.
Seidman, Harold. *Politics, Position, and Power: The Dynamics of Federal Organization.* New York: Oxford University Press, 1970.
Stanford Research Institute. *Human Resources Development for Oakland: Problems and Policies.* Menlo Park, Calif., 1968.
Stein, Harold, ed. *Public Administration and Policy Development: A Case Book.* New York: Harcourt Brace and Company, 1952.
Sundquist, James L., with the collaboration David W. Davis. *Making Federalism Work.* Washington, D.C.: The Brookings Institution, 1969.
Survey Research Center, University of California. *Poverty and Poverty Programs in Oakland.* Berkeley, 1967.
Talbot, Allan. *The Mayor's Game.* New York: Praeger, 1967.
Thompson, James D. *Organizations in Action.* New York: McGraw-Hill, 1967.
Waterston, Albert. *Development Planning: Lessons of Experience.* Baltimore: John Hopkins Press, 1965.
Wildavsky, Aaron. *Leadership in a Small Town.* Totowa, N.J.: Bedminster Press, 1964.
Young, James Sterling. *The Washington Community 1800-1828.* New York: Columbia University Press, 1966.
2. *Articles*
Allison, Graham T. and Morton H. Halperin, "Bureaucratic Politics: A Paradigm and Some Policy Implications." *World Politics* 24 (Spring 1972).

Almond, Gabriel A. "A Developmental Approach to Political Systems." *World Politics* 17 (January 1965).

Blumenthal, Richard. "Antipoverty and the Community Action Program." In *American Political Institutions and Public Policy*, edited by Allan P. Sindler. Boston: Little, Brown, 1969.

Dahl, Robert A. "The Concept of Power." *Behavioral Science* 2 (June 1957).

Deutsch, Karl W. "Social Mobilization and Political Development." *American Political Science Review* 55 (September 1961).

Elling, Ray H. and Sander Halebsky. "Organizational Differentiation and Support: A Conceptual Framework." *Administrative Science Quarterly* 6 (September 1961).

Evan, William M. "The Organization Set: Toward a Theory of Interorganizational Relations." In *Approaches to Organizational Design*, edited by James D. Thompson. Pittsburgh: University of Pittsburgh Press, 1966.

George, Alexander L. "Political Leadership and Social Change in American Cities." *Daedalus* 97 (Fall 1968).

Greenstein, Fred I. "The Impact of Personality on Politics: An Attempt to Clear Away Underbrush." *American Political Science Review* 61 (September 1967).

Harsanyi, John C. "Measurement of Social Power, Opportunity Costs, and the Theory of Two-Person Bargaining Games." *Behavioral Science* 7 (January 1962).

Holden, Matthew, Jr. " 'Imperialism' in Bureaucracy." *American Political Science Review* 60 (December 1966).

Huntington, Samuel P. "Political Development and Political Decay." *World Politics* 17 (April 1965).

Ilchman, Warren F. "A Political Economy of Foreign Aid: The Case of India." *Asian Survey* 7 (October 1967).

Jervis, Robert. "Hypotheses on Misperception." *World Politics* 24 (Spring 1972).

Levine, Sol and Paul E. White, "Exchange as a Conceptual Framework for the Study of Interorganizational Relationships." *Administrative Science Quarterly* 5 (March 1961).

Lipsky, Michael. "Protest as a Political Resource." *American Political Science Review* 62 (December 1968).

May, Judith. "Two Model Cities: Negotiations in Oakland." *Politics and Society* (Fall 1971).

Packenham, Robert A. "Approaches to the Study of Political Development." *World Politics* 17 (October 1964).

————. "Political Development Doctrines in the American Foreign Aid Program." *World Politics* 18 (January 1966).

Price, H. Douglas. Review of *Who Governs?* by Robert A. Dahl. *Yale Law Journal* 71 (1962).

Pye, Lucian W. "The Meaning of Political Development." *The Annals of the American Academy of Political and Social Science* 358 (March 1965).

Thompson, James D. and Arthur Tuden, "Strategies, Structure, and Processes of Organizational Decision." In *Comparative Studies in Administration*, edited by James D. Thompson. Pittsburgh: University of Pittsburgh Press, 1959.

Wilson, Woodrow. "The Study of Administration." Reprinted in *Political Science Quarterly* 56 (December 1941).

3. *Unpublished Papers*
Lockard, Duane. "Value, Theory, and Research in State and Local Politics." Paper delivered at the annual meeting of the American Political Science Association, 1970.
Mihaly, Eugene B. and Joan M. Nelson. "Political Development and U.S. Economic Assistance." Paper delivered at the annual meeting of the American Political Science Association, 1966.
Montgomery, Douglas G. "The Federal Delivery System: Impact on the Community. A Case Study of EDA and the West Oakland Health Center." Paper delivered at the annual meeting of the American Political Science Association, 1970.
Tendler, Judith. "Foreign Aid: A Study in Atypical Bureaucracy." University of California, Irvine, Department of Economics, 1970.
—-—. "The Abundance of Foreign Assistance" University of California, Irvine, Department of Economics, 1970.

4. *Government Documents*
Advisory Commission on Intergovernmental Relations. *Third Annual Report.* Washington, D.C., 1962.
City of Oakland. *Digest of Current Federal Programs in the City of Oakland.* Prepared for Mayor John H. Reading by Jeffrey L. Pressman, October, 1968.
Economic Opportunity Act of 1964.
Economic Opportunity Act, as amended 1967.
Oakland Task Force, Federal Executive Board. *An Analysis of Federal Decision-Making and Impact: The Federal Government in Oakland.* San Francisco, 1968; New York: Praeger, 1970.
Public Works and Economic Development Act of 1965.

5. *Newspapers*
The Montclarion
The New York Times
Oakland Tribune

Index